THE FEEL GOOD FACTORY ON

stress-free living

THE FEEL GOOD FACTORY ON
stress-free living

calm-spreading,
mind-soothing,
strain-slaying
ideas for a happy life

Feel Good Factory led by Elisabeth Wilson

MANUFACTURED BY
THE FEEL GOOD FACTORY

First published in 2009 by
Infinite Ideas Limited
36 St Giles
Oxford
OX1 3LD
United Kingdom
www.infideas.com

This edition published 2010 for Index Books Ltd

A CIP catalogue record for this book is available from the British Library

ISBN 978–1–906821–19–7

The publisher would like to thank Elisabeth Wilson and Jackee Holder for their
contributions to this book.

Designed and typeset by D.R. ink
Printed and bound in India by Replika Press Pvt. Ltd.

Contents

Two: Instant relief – a stress-free now
Calming techniques you can put into practice by bed time

Three: Regaining balance
Make that mythical work–life balance a reality

Four: Cherish yourself
Love yourself and life gets calm, serene, easier…

Introduction

We're all cracking up if you believe the statistics.
A recent survey discovered that 45% of women
said that their stress levels had risen during the
previous year, and that survey was carried out
before the credit crunch truly hit. The figures
are probably even higher now...

We're designed to cope with stress, of course – but that's one-off stressful events, not being permanently bathed in a soup of stress hormones. This sort of constant stress is just what is most dangerous for our health and well-being. Which is why stress-related health problems are on the way up, as is divorce. What is strange is that we seem to

Small changes make
a big difference

be 'hopeless and helpless' in face of the stress epidemic, unable to get ourselves out of it. It really doesn't take very much effort to instigate the changes that can mean you dispel stress on a daily basis and that's what this book is all about – dozens of ideas from experts on making your life a calmer, happier experience.

If your life is a bit overwhelming, making a few of these simple changes could mean that you sail through periods of stress, enjoying the thrill rather than hitting a wall. Small changes make a big difference and we believe you can make a big difference very quickly. Put one of these ideas into practice every day for 30 days, and keep building up your repertoire of soothing techniques and strategies and in just one month you will emerge a serener, more joyful, more sparkly version of you. Worth a few minutes a day, we think.

One
Back to basics

If you don't read anything else in
this book, read this.

You're the boss of you

Taking responsibility for your own life may be the toughest thing you do in your quest for inner peace. But the sooner you realise that you're your own knight in shining armour, the better.

There's a scene in the film *The Holiday* where Iris, the character played by Kate Winslet, realises an ultimate truth. Obviously, in her own life, she is the leading lady, but she's been conducting it as if she's in a supporting role. How many of us are doing that – allowing circumstances or other people to set the agenda for our lives so we feel the attention isn't on us? It's useful to remind yourself of it before you read any further, because ultimately none of these ideas will do any good unless you are prepared to make yourself a priority even if it's only for a few moments a day.

A survey carried out discovered that most of us *know* exactly what we need to do to combat stress and the illnesses that go along with it – we just don't do it. That's the problem.

If you are serious about becoming calm, be the boss of you

Just reading this book should prove to be a calming and soothing experience so if that's all that you have time for at the moment, read it and imagine yourself calm. But ultimately, if you are serious about becoming calm, be the boss of you, make the decision to live a calmer life.

The life you lead is the cumulative result of decisions that you have made and are constantly making. This is not to say that the outside world doesn't have any influence – of

Approaching a tedious task positively gives you back control of your life and that's the basis of calm

course it does – but ultimately you're running the show. You must not cave in to feeling powerless to make changes in your own life. While you may only have limited control over what you do, you can exercise full control over what you feel and how you react to those limitations.

Here's a typical example. Your boss decides to give you a report to do last thing on a Friday night and wants it first thing on Monday morning. It is probably not a practical response for you to jack in your job if your boss won't cut you some slack, but how you deal with a) the feelings this invokes in you and b) the actual task ahead can be vital to your sense of inner peace.

An unhelpful way to respond would be to stomp off home with the work, be in a bad mood all weekend and do it angrily and reluctantly, regularly sighing loudly and bemoaning your fate, while snapping at any poor family member silly enough to pass within a few feet of you.

A better way would be to accept that you've accepted the work, so you might as well do it well. Put on your favourite music, fix yourself something tasty to snack on and maybe

Feel good now: *Keep a time log of your working week so you finally get a realistic idea of how long it takes you to complete all your usual activities. This means you stop kidding yourself about how quickly you will perform tasks in an imperfect world where you're interrupted frequently.*

even get your partner to hang around in the same room so you have a feeling of companionship. Take regular breaks but, instead of breaking your flow by watching TV, go for a short walk, do some stretches or bang on some dance music and make some shapes. Approaching a tedious task in this way gives you back control of your life and that's the basis of calm.

It is really easy to lose sight of the fact that we always are in control of what we feel, and thus can always stay calm if we choose to. Society is organised in a very complex way and one of the side effects of this organisation is to make you feel very small and insignificant. If we want to buy a house, most of us have to get a mortgage. To get a mortgage we need to get a job. To get the partner you want, you have to be attractive, be it in looks or behaviour. You have to continue to attract if you want to retain your partner. Let's not even start on the demands of the children if you have them. In short, it can very quickly seem as if everyone has got a vested interest in your life. You can feel trapped and controlled by the social restrictions. But ultimately, this is self-defeating. Remember, you do have control. You are free to make your own decisions.

The real revolution happens when you realise that the social restrictions are your own construct. You have made this. You have decided you want this house or that job. Your choice of partner is determined by you. Even your aggravating mother is in your life because you allow her to be there. As such, if you are feeling unhappy and conflicted by any aspect of your life, you can change it. Feel that power. Now when you read these ideas, believe that you can follow them and turn your world around. You are the leading lady of your life. And if you want calm, you can create it.

Quiz:
who is in control of your life?

Put a tick next to the response that most applies to you.

If you want a job well done, do it yourself.

Agree   Not sure   Disagree

I am fine on my own for long periods of time.

Agree   Not sure   Disagree

You make your own luck in life.

Agree   Not sure   Disagree

If I set my mind on something, I know I'll get it.

Agree   Not sure   Disagree

If someone tries to manipulate me, I almost do the opposite as a reflex.

Agree   Not sure   Disagree

I don't pay much attention to compliments or insults.

Agree   Not sure   Disagree

I hardly ever spend time working to other people's needs.

Agree   Not sure   Disagree

Score 2 points for every 'agree', 1 point for every 'not sure' and 0 for a 'disagree'.

8 or more

You feel you are in total charge of your life and now that you have decided to seek calm, shouldn't have any trouble making those changes.

5-7

You feel moderately in control but should guard against other people taking up your time.

4 or under

You feel powerless fairly often. Think about saying 'no' more often and thinking of yourself.

Find an hour a day to play

Shut your eyes, breathe deeply. Picture how much better you'd feel about today if there was a whole hour that you knew you could spend doing exactly what you wanted...

Practically everything we want to do with our time can be divided into two main categories:

- The stuff we yearn to do because it's relaxing or fun. In this group is lying in bed watching a movie or meeting a girlfriend for an impromptu drink.
- The stuff that's prefixed in our brain with the words 'ought to', 'should', 'must'. We know the rewards are worth it, but this category doesn't always make our heart sing. In this group is going for a run or quality time with the kids.

We want to do both and we need to find time for both but both categories tend to get shunted to the sidelines because there always seems to be more time tomorrow for this stuff. Our bed, the movie, the park and the kids aren't going anywhere, whereas that report has to be done NOW.

But of course, that is just an illusion. The great irony is that the activities that have to be done NOW are all too often the ephemera of our lives, the things that don't really matter. Whereas the important stuff, looking after our mental and physical well-being, fostering good relationships, being around just to hang out with the kids are the important 'soul' tasks. Quite simply the stuff that makes life worth living.

Ask yourself, if you don't find time for these things, how will you feel in five years' time? More to the point, how will you look? What will be your regrets?

OK, let's not get too heavy, but nothing in your life will change unless you take action. If you don't take the time to exercise, if you consistently allow family and work demands to be more important than your good health, then at best you'll be more vulnerable to illness; at worst, you'll be fat (and still be more vulnerable to illness).

There is one other really good reason to start prioritising some of the stuff in these two categories. When you spend at least a bit of time doing the things that you want to do, you will feel that you are in control and that is probably the number one de-stressor.

How to do this

Get out your diary and write down everything you're expected to make happen in the next month. This could take some time. Include everything from work projects, organising babysitters, buying birthday presents, decorating the bathroom, taxing the car, medical appointments.

OK, finished? Right, go through the list and mark the items

that you can delegate to someone else. Be honest. These are the items you can delegate, not the ones that no one else will want to do or those that no one else will do as well as you. Don't worry, you don't have to hand over all these tasks. Just 10% of them.

Now you've off-loaded 10% of your work for the next month, think about dumping 10% of what you have to do every day. Jot down your tasks for tomorrow. Quickly without thinking too much, run through them marking each entry

A. Must do
B. Should do
C. Could do

Now knock two of the Bs of the list, and three of the Cs. Be honest. Many Cs can be put off until another day; by then they may reach B or even A status, and that's fine. You'll do them when you have to. Replace them with an hour of some activity that you know would de-stress you or add value to your life. Mark it with a whacking great 'A'. Pencil it in your diary. Good times for this are: first thing in the morning (if you forgot the ironing, you could go to bed an hour earlier and find an hour to read a favourite novel in bed with a cup of tea); as soon as you get home from work (kick off your shoes and head straight to bed for a nap or to the park for a run); or as soon as the kids are in bed (don't slump in front of the TV, disappear into the garden with your iPod and a glass of wine).

Soon, giddy with success, you'll be prioritising yourself every single day. You'll realise that much on that 'to do' list doesn't have to be done or will simply disappear if you ignore it, but you won't care, because you'll be living a life. You will have learned the most important lesson, that life is really too short to wallow in your own personal C-list – feeling busy but achieving nothing that matters.

The golden rule of relaxation

We're designed to get stressed. It's how we deal with it that's the problem.

Why are we facing an epidemic of stress? The answer lies in the way we interpret the word 'relax'. Remember that stress developed in order for us to deal with danger. When faced with something that scares us (more likely nowadays to be a 'to-do' list running into double figures rather than the sabre-toothed tigers that threatened our ancestors), we release adrenaline. This in turn causes the release of noradrenaline and cortisol and these three hormones working together sharpen our wits, release energy to our muscles and divert resources from the parts of the body that don't need it to the parts that do – your limbs rather than your gut, which is why you feel twitchy when you're stressed and can't sit still. The adrenaline coursing through your body is urging you to fight or run away.

But that reaction is designed to work for a very short period of time. The extreme stress response helps save your life

Feel good now: *Pick one day next week to be your day to do whatever you want. Plan it in detail and relish the anticipation. On no account cancel it.*

and even back in the Neolithic age, our ancestors usually only had to save their lives occasionally. After a period of intense stress, fighting the aforementioned tiger or killing a mammoth, our ancestors would loaf around staring at their fire – rest and recreation, calm and peace, lots of sleep – sometimes for days. Rest is essential to repair and recover

Rest is essential to repair and recover from the effect of stress hormones in our bodies

from the effect of stress hormones in our bodies. That's what we learned to expect over the course of millennia.

What's going wrong in twenty-first-century life is that we are triggering the stress response more often and our methods of relaxation are not as effective. Think of how we relax after a stressful day. We are likeliest to celebrate with alcohol, a cigarette, coffee (all of which trigger the stress response). And that is if we bother to relax at all. After a stressful situation, we throw ourselves straight into another one. This means that our bodies are bathed in stress hormones for far longer than was ever intended.

The body's hormones work in delicate balance. When the three main stress hormones are fired they affect the levels of all the others (notably insulin which regulates sugar levels and energy) and serotonin (the happy hormone which affects mood and sleep). When they go awry over long periods of time, the results can be disastrous for our health, both mental and physical. Which is why we start off stressed and end up stressed, fat, unhappy and unhealthy.

The solution is simple: build relaxation into your life, hour by hour, day by day.

5 minutes every hour

See your day not as a long purgatory of stress but as lots of small stress responses punctuated with mini-relaxation breaks. As a rough rule, every waking hour should have five minutes of pleasure. So after every hour of working, take a minimum to do something pleasurable – call a friend, stretch your shoulders, have a cup of green tea. Can't leave your desk? Spend a few minutes daydreaming of something that makes you happy.

15 minutes every day

Practise active relaxation – listening to music, yoga, sex, dancing. TV is passive and doesn't count.

3 hours every week

At least three hours every week should be spent doing an activity you love. It should be calming and non-work orientated. For die-hard perfectionists, one useful rule of thumb when deciding on your activity is that it only counts as your 'three hours' if you could do it without wearing make-up – in other words, it doesn't count if it involves people judging you. You will know yourself if your activity is truly relaxing. Be honest. This cannot be an activity that furthers your career, your ambitions, your children's friendships or your perfectionist streak.

Two
Instant relief – a stress-free now

Calming techniques you can put into
practice by bed time.

The de-stress kit: don't leave home without it...

Put together a toolkit of a few favourite remedies
which help you feel calm in seconds.
Keep it near you.

Aromatherapy

The great advantage of aromatherapy is that it helps
you achieve equilibrium in minutes. That and its instant
portability. Look for opportunities throughout your day to
insert a mini-treatment. Carry a hankie with a few drops of
peppermint oil on it to clear your mind and aid concentration.
When showering, cover the plughole with a flannel and add
4-6 drops of a combination of essential oils to the shower tray.
Add one drop of essential oil to your existing moisturiser.
Inhale deeply as you apply it. Soak your feet in a bowl of
water scented with pine when you're watching TV. Put a
couple of drops of essential oil into the middle of a hot wet
flannel, wring it out, hold it over your face and breathe deeply.

Best oils for calm

Lavender: great for peaceful feelings and helping you drift
off to sleep

Geranium: gives a sense of being in control

Grapefruit: good for when you're feeling low

Cedarwood: helps when you are anxious or stressed

Clary sage: when you're feeling put upon and resentful (but
not if you're pregnant)

Rose: when your emotions are jangled

Chamomile: comforting and deeply relaxing

Neroli: melts away anxiety

Flower remedies

Bach Rescue Remedy is the famous flower essence that has helped generations calm down fast – it's even said to work on pets. The flower remedy business is booming so search on the Internet for others. A few drops of these under your tongue throughout the day are a wonderful 'prop' against stress.

Vitamin C

Did you know that vitamin C has a similar effect on the system as coffee but without the negative jitteriness. When you want some instant sparkle, dissolve some soluble vitamin C tablets in a glass of water and throw it down. It should give you enthusiasm and energy within minutes.

Bubblewrap

Don't laugh but studies have shown that bursting the bubbles on bubble wrap works really well to melt away pent up nervous energy and release muscle tension.

Instant ideas to slow you down fast

- *Take off your watch. Work to your own agenda*

- *Leave a hole in your diary every day of the week. Use these gaps to relax*

- *Set your alarm 15 minutes early and lie in bed*

- *Plant some bulbs or herbs*

- *Close your eyes: breathe in, breathe out. Do this nine times as often as you remember*

- *If you can't cook an entire meal from scratch, peel a carrot, toss a salad or steam some broccoli to eat with your ready-meal*

- *Bathe rather than shower*

- *Stand on the escalators rather than walk*

- *Take the bus rather than drive. Use the time to read a book or just stare out of the window*

- *Swap instant coffee for green tea. It's only the power of suggestion that makes you feel more Zen, but it works*

Calm body – work with nature not against it

This is the very quickest way to calm down when you're stressed out.

When you're stressed, what do you do? Grab a coffee, have a cigarette, vent to your girlfriend? All of these are the result of adrenaline and cortisol ripping around your body, making you very twitchy. The result of this is that you want a fight or you want to run away. The trouble is that just about every response we have to stress is guaranteed to wind us up even more (see above, all of which increase, rather than decrease, the hormones that initiate the stress response). This means that in extreme cases, some of us live in an almost permanent state of arousal – and not in a good way – our bodies permanently on standby for trouble.

Use the exercise as a way of solving your problems

But this is not what nature intended. The 'fight or flight' response, like all hormonal response is meant to be run through fairly quickly. You can burn off the hormones in a matter of minutes if you give your body what it's craving – a fight or a good run. In other words, get physical. Next time you're stressed, grab your coat and get outside. You'll find that the stress is dispersed in no time at all as the hormones disappear.

Take it outside

You can simply go for a walk, but once the initial stress has gone, use the exercise as a way of solving your problems. Once you're out there with the air and wind, set your focus. Set the agenda by walking with a question in mind. Hold your questions gently in your thoughts and get on with enjoying your walk. Do the same with something that you're worrying about. Most people find that they return from walking with stress gone and a clear mind. Remember the words of St Augustine – *Solvitur Ambulando* – it is solved by walking.

Feel good now: *If you wake in the night, don't lie awake becoming frustrated. Read for 20 minutes to see if it helps you doze off. But invest in a reading torch. Putting on a light can trigger the 'wake up' centres in your brain.*

Gently does it

Practise what the Buddhists refer to as Loving Kindness.
Think of it as your creative comfort food. Perhaps in
your early years no one came to your rescue. When we
were children we may not have had anyone to soothe our
wounds or take care of our damaged egos so now, as the
adult, it is your job to do the taking care of. Items on my
list of small acts of kindness and tenderness include:

1. *A hot bath with oils or sea salts*
2. *Spending an hour or more reading for pleasure*
3. *Solo trips to the cinema, museums, galleries, book readings*
4. *Buying organic foods for dinner*
5. *Spending a Saturday afternoon watching DVDs*
6. *Lunch at the weekend with friends*

Now make a list of your own kindness treats and apply
when you feel like some TLC.

Calm mind – instant clarity

On days when you are feeling overwhelmed by the sheer nuttiness of your life, keep a list of these questions in your purse. Answering them will bring instant clarity.

Zapping daily problems

The 'best use' question is invaluable in negotiating your way through those days when there are numerous calls on your time. It is the quickest way to prioritise 'on the run', sometimes quite ruthlessly. On the morning of a manic day decide what you've got to achieve that day. If anything interrupts ask yourself 'is this the best use of my time right now?' If the answer's no, take a rain-check and come back to it later. So if a friend calls at work, nine times out of ten, you won't chat then, you'll call her back at a more convenient time – unless, of course, she is very upset about something, then talking to her is the best use of your time. Nothing else is more important. That way you don't let colleagues sidetrack you with complaints unless of course it's the best use of your time.

Solving bigger issues – looking for the miracle

Solution therapy is a way of resolving a problem or crisis quickly. When faced with a problem, ask yourself:

If all my problems and worries had disappeared how would I know a miracle had happened. What tangible changes would there be in my life?

How would I behave differently?

How would my family and friends behave differently towards me?

What changes would family and friends see in my behaviour as a result of the change?

Are there parts of the miracle that are already happening?

How have you made these things happen? How could you make more of them happen?

On a scale of zero to 10 where zero is the worst that you have ever been and 10 is 'miracle', where would you be now?

How could you move up a notch? How would others know that you had moved up a notch by the changes in you?

Answering these questions helps you focus on positive action you can take to help yourself, and leads you to behaviours that allow you to act 'as if' you had found solutions to your problems. As we now know acting 'as if' you have found a solution is a great way to make them actually happen.

Never lose your keys again

If you've noticed an increase in frequency of memory lapses, your multi-tasking lifestyle could be to blame. The 'fight or flight' response actually sharpens your cognitive abilities. But chronic stress over long periods of time is a different matter. If your mind is bustling ahead to deal with the day's problems, it's concentrating on other things and you're not noticing what's going around you. Not surprisingly, you can't retrieve memories of what you did today because your mind was actually living in tomorrow.

Repeat, repeat

The answer is to stand back and observe yourself and have enough insight to recognise that you are stressed and that is going to affect your memory. When you're busy and stressed, you're not taking in information in the same way and you're not going to be able to recall it. Make like a boy scout and be prepared. On a busy day when you meet someone new, be aware that you are more likely to forget their name. Make more effort than usual during introductions. Repeat a new name inside your head. Use it again in conversation as soon as you can. This repetition is important. When learning anything new during a stressed period, repeat it to yourself and if possible say it out loud three or four times, increasing the amount of time between each repetition. This 'repetition, pause, repetition' pattern strengthens memory.

This technique also works for items or tasks that you have to remember – and always forget. If you're fed up going to the supermarket to buy tomatoes and coming back with everything else but tomatoes, try the above. If it doesn't work, then simply don't rely on your memory. Write everything down in a notebook you keep with you.

Routine actions will cause memory problems if you do them differently every day. The very fact that we do some things over and over again can make them easy to forget. That's because when you put items you use frequently in different places from one day to the next, you have to block the memory of what you did with them yesterday and the day before in order to find them today. Which is why it seems you've spent half your life looking for your keys and purse.

Create a memory pot

*Place a bowl or basket near your front door where
everything goes as soon as you get home, and which you
check before you leave the house. This is not as simple
as it sounds – it takes about two or three weeks before it
becomes second nature. And even then, it makes sense to
keep a spare set of keys somewhere separately.*

Cut anxiety

*The phenomenon of worrying endlessly if you've done
something that you've done a hundred times before is
down to something called 'social misattribution', the
fancy name for recalling the action but not realising
that you performed it on another occasion. Again, it's
because you're not focusing on the action while you're
doing it.*

*The answer is to take the time to check what you're
wearing. As your arm reaches out to switch off the iron,
note 'wearing a blue shirt'. When you get the doubt
that you've done an action, recall what your arm was
wearing when you did it. Look down. Blue shirt. Check.
On you go with your day. It takes about two to three
weeks for this to work.*

What was I saying?

The horrible experience of losing the thread of what you're saying mid-sentence is called 'state-dependent retrieval' which means when you're stressed out, your physiology changes in such a way that it's difficult to hold onto your thoughts. If this affects you when you are giving presentations, the only way to help yourself is to be so well prepared that you don't get so stressed. If it strikes during everyday conversations, then it could be that you are jumping ahead to solve future problems so that you are not staying in the 'now' and concentrating on the conversation. Do your best to stay with one issue at a time.

A ten-minute yoga routine

This is a simple yoga routine that stretches muscles – back, shoulders, face – that carry tension. It has the advantage that each move is carried out on the floor, which is handy when you've had a long day.

Five reasons to take up yoga

Those who practise yoga regularly report that the calming benefits follow them around all day. Here are some proven reasons to consider it

- *It slows weight gain. Those over the age of 45 who do yoga regularly are 8lbs lighter than those who don't*
- *Yoga eases pain*
- *It induces sleep. Expect benefits after three months*
- *It decreases stress. One class a week reduces the stress hormone cortisol*
- *Yoga keeps skin young. It reduces the breakdown of the skin's scaffolding, collagen, in just 10 days.*

To release tension in the shoulders and back

The spinal twist

Lie on your back, knees bent, feet on the floor, hip-width apart. Take your arms out to the sides, rotating the shoulders, arms, palms upwards. Keep the arms relaxed on the floor with the hands a little lower than the shoulders.

Exhale and roll your hips so your lower body falls to the right while you roll the neck and head to the left. Inhale returning to centre, and exhale again while you repeat the action to the other side. Continue with this five times to each side.

To stretch out kinks in your back

The cat pose

Kneel on all fours, with your wrists below your shoulders and your knees below your hips so that the arms and thighs are vertical and parallel. Spread the hands and fingers wide, middle fingers pointing straight forwards. Point the feet and toes so that the fronts of the ankles are stretching along the floor. Exhale and pull in your pelvis and abdominal area, round the back like a cat until your head is down and you are looking backwards. Hold the posture and inhale, pushing your tail bone away, stretching into the buttocks and slowly extending the movement so that your spine arches down. Lift your head gently with a smile. Continue stretching deeply and slowly in each direction with the breath.

To deeply relax and calm

Child's pose

Sit on your heels and slowly bend forwards to rest your

forehead on the floor, or on a pillow. The arms are relaxed on the floor alongside the body with the palms turned upwards and elbows softening outwards. Relax your body and stay like this for as long as you can, listening to your breathing.

To reduce tension in the shoulders and increase blood flow to brain

Downward-facing dog

Get on to your hands and knees as you did for the Cat Pose. Curl your toes under and breathe in as you take your knees off the floor so that you are on your hands and toes. As you exhale, stretch the spine backwards and upwards away from your hands, allowing your head to come towards the floor as your buttocks stretch up towards the ceiling. Focus on releasing into the shoulders as you move towards an inverted 'V' shape, with a straight back and straight legs. Push your heels down towards the floor as far as you can. Go back into the Child's Pose and rest.

To totally relax

The corpse pose

Lie flat on your back with legs comfortably apart and your arms hanging loosely with palms turned up. Be quite still and concentrate on your breath.

Every breath you take… is another opportunity to create calm

Your sense of smell is rooted in one of the very oldest parts of the brain from an evolutionary point of view. The limbic area is connected with memory, emotion and sleep. And, with a little know-how, all of these centres can be 'triggered' in order to boost your energy.

Scent is inhaled via millions of sensitive cells that line the nasal passages and these send messages straight to the brain. Which means that the response is near instantaneous.

Scent will work for you without any conscious thought of your own, which is why it's such a useful tool. In spring, a bowl of strongly scented hyacinths on your desk will help you get through a difficult day more smoothly. In summer, lying on a newly mown lawn for 10 minutes will energise you faster than coffee, and in autumn, burning apple logs

In summer, lying on a newly mown lawn for 10 minutes will energise you faster than coffee

if you're lucky enough to have an open fire will lift your spirits. Pine-scented candles in winter evoke the very spirit of Christmas. The power of certain smells to make us feel better instantly is one of the arguments used for collective consciousness – the idea that we are all linked by common ancestral memories.

You can take it a step further by buying a few aromatherapy oils for everyday use. Smell is such a powerful sense that if you associate a certain aroma with a particular emotion, then every time you smell that smell, you'll feel the same emotion. You can use this to your advantage. If you want an instant relaxant, sniff a scent when you are calm and happy (on holiday is good). Whenever you smell it from then on, you'll be taken back to that calm and happy place. Lavender, may chang or geranium are good for this and all are renowned for their uplifting and de-stressing power.

Of course, the very simplest relaxing tool of all is to rely on your breath to calm you down. Yogic breathing has been shown in some studies to 'wake up' your brain especially the parts responsible for creativity and logical thinking. Close off your right nostril with the thumb of your right hand and breathe in through your left for the count of four. Now close off your left nostril with the index finger of your right hand and exhale for the count of four. Breathe in through your right nostril, and then out through your left, closing off your right nostril with your thumb. Repeat half a dozen times. This is great for relaxing you at any time of the day.

Quiz:
Do you take the time to recreate?

Recreation is just that: the chance to recreate yourself. But so many of us are so busy that we never take time out. And the result is a flattening of life, a feeling that we're losing out. And we are: without the chance to recreate we risk losing our equilibrium, bounce and sparkle.

Write yes or no beside each of the statements below. Score 1 for every 'yes', and 0 for every 'no'.

- You take a breather every few hours during your working day _____
- Your work doesn't impinge on your personal life _____
- You see plenty of the friends that matter _____
- You see plenty of the people that raise

56

your spirit _____

- You have time at least once a week to act spontaneously – catch a movie, savour a cup of coffee at a pavement café, phone a friend just because they crossed your mind _____
- You read books as opposed to magazines, newspapers or work-related reading _____
- You leave work at a reasonable time each day _____
- You always take all of your holiday allowance _____
- You always take a full hour for lunch unless there's a real emergency _____
- You always have time if a friend needs half an hour _____

7 or more

You do have time for yourself and you probably feel there is enough time to follow your interests, plan your future and be creative with your options.

6 or less

You need to slow down a little more to give your brain and body a chance to recover from the hectic pace of your life.

Restoration day

Book yourself a day out. By tomorrow, you will
feel rested, stronger and more in control.

All you need is 24 hours. If you have children ask someone else to look after them for as much of the day as possible. Remember that if you don't look after yourself, you will have nothing left to give to others. It is best to follow a 'schedule' than lie in bed all day.

The restoration day is based on three principles:

- Replenishing your body by giving it a rest
- Resting your brain by focusing on your body
- Nourishing yourself with healthy, simple food which will replenish the nutrients stripped away by stress

Before you get up

When you wake, acknowledge that this day will be different. Today you are going to shift the emphasis onto relaxation and releasing tension, and replace what stress has drained away from your body. Stretch. If you feel like it, turn over and go back to sleep. If not, read an inspirational book – self-help, poetry, a favourite novel. Don't reach for your usual coffee or tea. Sip a mug of hot water with lemon. This according to naturopaths boosts the liver which has to work hard processing what goes into our body. And even if your diet is perfect, hot lemon water is very soothing. Every time panic hits because you're not doing anything – now and for the rest of the day – breathe in deeply for a count of eight and out for a count of eight.

When you get up

Stretch for 10 minutes. A few yoga stretches are good, but it doesn't matter as long as you try to stretch every muscle in your body. You don't have to do this 'perfectly', it's not a workout, it's a reminder. You have a body: it carries tension and pain. Feel the cricks draining out. Finish with the yoga position known as the Child's Pose. Kneel with your legs tucked under you. Bend forward so your forehead rests as near to the floor as possible in front of you. A cushion under your knees might make this more comfortable. Take your arms behind you with hands pointing back and palms upward. Rest like this and breathe deeply. This releases tension in the neck and shoulders which is where many of us store it.

Breakfast

Try a smoothie: blend a cup of natural yogurt with one banana and couple of handfuls of sweet fruits; peach, mango, strawberries, pineapple. Thin if preferred with a little fruit juice. Sip slowly, preferably outside. Imagine the vitamin C zooming around your body replacing the levels depleted by stress. My advice today is to eat lightly and avoid (except for the odd treat) foods that strain digestion too much. Drink coffee and tea if you normally do – the last thing you want is caffeine withdrawal headaches – but don't have more than three caffeine drinks. It makes you jittery even if you are very used to it, but you have just come to accept those jangled nerves as your normal state.

Morning

Get outside and as near to nature as you can manage. Ideally, lie on your back on the grass. Stare at the sky. Let your mind drift off. Or walk in the countryside, the park, sit in your garden. If you really can't bear to be still, do some gardening. Do not let the weather or the season put you off. Be aware today of the weather whatever that may be. If it is inclement, return home and get cosy in front of a fire, sleeping or reading or listening to music, but no television or computer screens. The idea is to feel yourself sinking into relaxation, not numbing out.

Lunch

Have a huge salad combining every colour of vegetable you can think of – green, yellow, orange, purple, red. More vitamin C. Serve with a delicious dressing. This meal must include one absolute treat – a glass of wine, a dish of ice cream, a piece of chocolate. Lie back and really taste it.

Afternoon

Go back to bed. Or curl up in a corner of your sofa. Watch a favourite film. A weepie might work well for you. A good cry can be therapeutic if you have been carrying stress linked to disappointment or sadness. But crying is strictly restricted to a two-hour period this afternoon. Then put negative thoughts aside and 'come back to the present', concentrate that right now, no matter what else is going on in your life, you are safe and well. You have the potential to enjoy the rest of the day. Focusing on negative thoughts will only diminish the healing power of the day.

Dinner

Eat another vegetable-based meal: a salad or a stir-fry, following the 'eat a rainbow' advice above. Have a piece of fish grilled in a little oil or butter if you like. Think delicious but simple. Present your food beautifully, eat by candlelight. Relish the tastes.

And so to bed

Go to bed early, preferably by 9.30 p.m. Resist the temptation to watch TV. Read, listen to gentle music.

Tame your to-do list

The problem with to-do lists is that it takes
seconds to scribble yet another entry – which
calms you down for that fraction of a second.
But if you never get round to doing it, it will
stress you out even more.

The secret to a successful to-do list is to allocate time to complete the tasks.

Try instead the ideas of work days, buffer days and free days. Everything you need to do falls into one of these three categories.

Work days: self explanatory

Free days: fun days and these should be a complete break from work. These are for rest and recreation, and if you don't think there is time for this, remember recreation is just that – the time to recreate, and what you're recreating is yourself. If you don't have at least one of these a week, you will struggle to remain calm.

Buffer days: these are so-called because they act as a buffer against stress. These are the days you get on top of all those little things that need to get done – filing receipts, updating your CV. These are never as important as other things – until your tax return is due tomorrow or you lose your job. Buffer days are those times when you stress-proof your life in advance.

Step 1

Prepare the master list. You need a notebook in which you write down everything that needs doing – now and in the future, important and unimportant.

Step 2

OK, now you have your list, divide it into two. You can do this with two different coloured marker pens. More than half will be stuff you have to do by a definite date (insuring the car, finishing a work project) and the rest will be the wish list, stuff you'd like to do in an ideal world (sorting out your photos, getting started on your tax return).

Step 3

Now get your calendar. You can use your diary, but a calendar that shows a month on a page works better. First mark off the free days (remember one a week minimum). Then the work days and finally buffer days. Or it may have to be a buffer morning or evening – when we're busy it's difficult to allocate time to administration, but aim for a concentrated three hours if you want to get anything useful done. Decide on the top five things on your must-do list – some will be work, some will be buffer. Schedule these in on your calendar at the next appropriate session. Colour coding helps you see at a glance when your life is getting out of balance. Devise your own system or you can use mini post-it notes in three colours for each kind of day, write each separate task on the appropriate colour and slam it on the correct day.

Step 4

Look at your wish list. Pick three things on it. These will probably fall into buffer or free days. If you look forward to it with unalloyed pleasure, it's for a free day. If there is any element of duty whatsoever, it's a buffer. Scribble these on appropriate colour-coded post-it notes and bang them on the calendar. Every evening rip off the post-it notes for the next day and transfer them to your diary, sling them in the bin when you've finished the task (very satisfying). Any not finished can be allotted another slot. If you don't use post-it notes, just scribble the items for the next day into your diary.

What have you achieved besides a multicoloured calendar bristling with post-it notes? A lot. You have prioritised your time and you've allocated all the urgent things a time slot. You've also prioritised some of the non-urgent ones, and most importantly found time for yourself.

Calming rituals

**Look to the East for some simple calming rituals
that you can undertake in seconds.**

A quick yoga move to energise and calm

This move, the 'Salute to the Sun', is designed to be carried out while facing the rising sun. Master it, and it will serve you well, delivering instant energy and alertness benefits. Don't do it at night – it could keep you awake.

Stand straight and tall, feet bare and about a foot apart. Hold your hands, pointing upwards in front of your chest as if you were praying.

Inhale and lift your arms straight above your head, stretching backwards a few inches so that you feel a stretch across your front.

Exhale. At the same time, bend forward from your hips so that your hands are on each side of your feet. You may have to bend your legs slightly at the knee until you get more flexible.

Inhale. At the same time, place your right foot behind you as far as you can. Then place your left foot there, too, so that your hands and feet are supporting your body.

Exhale. At the same time, lower your knees to the floor, then your chest, then your chin. You should look as if you are about to do a push-up.

Inhale. At the same time, slowly straighten your arms and arch your back from the waist so your chest is lifted off the floor.

Exhale.

At the same time, push back onto your knees, tuck your toes in, then straighten your arms and legs so that you make an inverted V, standing on your toes.

Inhale and step between your hands with your left foot.

Exhale and step between your hands with your right foot.

Inhale. At the same time, slowly return to the standing position.

Now, repeat. Take your time to learn how to do this correctly. The breathing is important. But with practice you should be able to do this between 10 and 20 times in a minute. The more you do it, the more benefits you receive. Once you've got the hang of it, swap the leg you lead with from stage 3, right first, then left.

You should feel energised and calm afterwards because, according to the yogis, all the upward and downward movement stimulates the adrenal glands.

A Japanese bath to soothe and calm

Try this once a week – it is more restful than a simple candlelit bath and can work wonders mid-week, on a 'school night', when you are beginning to unravel. The Japanese bath has cumulative effects, the more you do it, the more powerfully it works. There is a set pattern to it and the predictability is soothing in itself.

You will need: a balancing essential oil such as lavender or geranium or frankincense, an aromatherapy burner, a quiet place to sit, a clean bathroom (free of clutter), some soft towels (preferably warmed), a loofah or a body brush or sisal glove, a small bowl, comfortable clothes, a teapot, cup, strainer, loose-leafed tea, a candle, a blanket, and a minimum of one hour.

First, light the burner in the bathroom, lock the door and sit there quietly breathing in the fragrance, letting your mind quieten and be still. Lay your hands on your stomach, breathe in deeply and feel your stomach move out. Breathe out and feel your stomach contracting. Let go of all other thoughts. Keep your focus on your senses. Let anxious thoughts drift away with the fragrance.

Undress and gently draw a brush or loofah over your body working towards the heart. Then step into the shower – it works best if it is a slightly cooler temperature than usual. Lather up and get clean. Imagine the events of the day washing down the plughole so that you emerge as new. Now run yourself a hot bath. Add a few drops of your balancing oil. Sink into the bath and let thoughts drift away with the steam. When properly relaxed, use the small bowl to ladle water all over your body. Focus your mind on pouring the water as gracefully as you can. Study the pattern of the falling water; if you feel like you're in a trance, good.

When calm and centred, emerge, wrapped in your warm towel. Dress in your comfortable clothing.

Go to a peaceful corner of your home and light a candle (if you can do this whole ritual by candlelight it is doubly restful). Then make some tea, holding the mindful state and making movements graceful. Green tea gives the authentic feel but any tea will do. Finally retire to your quiet place, wrap yourself in the blanket, sip your tea, inhaling the fragrance. Focus on the candle flame, keep your attention on it. Imagine any anxious thoughts drifting away in the fragrant steam rising from your cup

Spirituality in seconds

Prayers are a way of connecting with something greater than ourselves, and that can be very relaxing...

There have been a number of scientific studies into the power of prayer. One of the most famous was a double-blind study that was conducted at the San Francisco General Hospital's Coronary Care Unit in the 1980s. Patients were selected at random by a computer to receive prayer from a group of individuals as well as additional prayer from folks not connected to the study. The patients, doctors and even the scientist conducting the study were not told which had been selected. They found that the group selected for prayer, in comparison to the control group, had much better health, needed less medication or resuscitation and suffered far fewer deaths. This was true whether or not the recipient believed in God or not.

Some scientists believe that it is the sense of being in a community that cares about you that causes prayer to be so healing. Indeed in the shamanic tradition, there is a group healing that is sometimes done when one person really needs a massive amount of healing for something serious. A group of shamans will 'journey' to bring back healing for the person in question. However this doesn't explain why prayer also works when the person being prayed for has no idea this is being done for them.

Even fungi and seeds that are prayed for do better than those that aren't, and they can't be responding to a placebo.

Praying for those in our circle who could do with some support is a very restful and gracious act. Light a candle and meditate in front of it while thinking of the outcomes you'd like to achieve for the people on your prayer list.

Another way of spreading blessings around is to each day put a few coppers in a jar, maybe some silver on days you're feeling flush. When the jar is full, take it all down to your favourite charity and donate it. Then start again. This daily practice gives you a sense of grace as, when you donate it, you'll be answering someone else's prayers somewhere.

Another way to find calm is to discover a sacred place for you. Visit it when no one is likely to be there. It could be a church – visit it when no one else is there. You don't need to do anything. Just sit, enjoy the atmosphere built up over years of specialness and sacred peace. It could be a tranquil natural beauty spot or any other building that fills you with peace.

Wish yourself calm

'Happy talk' can be your new best friend.

The legendary American wit, Dorothy Parker, on hearing a telephone ring, apparently drawled, 'What fresh hell is this?' On really busy days, we've all felt like that. Sometimes we're almost scared to answer the phone or open our emails in case there are more demands being made of us. That can get us into a victim mentality that is completely unhelpful

Sometimes we're almost scared to answer the phone or open our emails in case there are more demands being made of us

in moving through our day. There is a simple technique that once mastered can help you deal with difficult days with equanimity.

Develop a mantra to suit whatever crisis you're in today and that you say to yourself every time your mind goes into tailspin. A good one is, 'I am serenely gliding towards my goal and everything is complete.' Another is, 'I have plenty of time to do everything I need to get done.' This will create vast swathes of time in your previously manic day. Try chanting these every time panic strikes. Doing this out loud works particularly well.

This is an example of 'positive affirmation'. The theory, hokey though it sounds, is that by putting out the positive message, the universe responds by giving you what you ask for. It responds to your intention, even if it's not strictly true as you say it. Even if you don't believe that, you will find that saying peaceful words calms you down. What is indisputable is, if you try this on a regular basis, you will see a difference in your life.

Affirmations should always be in the present tense. Avoid those along the lines of, 'I will get on top of my filing' as this implies that you will always be about to get on top of your filing, and never actually succeed.

It also helps to include words like 'serene' or 'calm' or 'abundant' or 'sparkling' – words that lift you emotionally. They make you feel happier and the happier you are when you affirm, the sooner the magic happens.

Don't be too specific, give the universe some freedom of movement. For instance you will get better results with, 'I am romantically cherished and loved and I return that love,' than, 'Paul White of 14 Acacia Avenue loves me.' Trust that if Paul is The One, he'll respond to the first affirmation; and if you're not too specific, the universe may surprise you with someone even better.

Avoid negatives – that means avoiding 'I am free from pain' as the universe is literalist. Your focus there is on the word 'pain' without seeing the context of 'free from'. It would be better to say 'I am happy and healthy,' as presumably you wouldn't be very happy and healthy if you were in pain.

Say your affirmation all the time, if possible, under your breath. Every couple of hours repeat your mantra out loud. You can put it on your screen saver or a note on your desk if you don't mind people knowing what you're up to. Saturate yourself with the words. Remember you don't have to believe this for it to work. Keep persevering.

Oprah Winfrey's steps to calm

She nips problems in the bud

'For years I've noticed that the universe speaks to us in whispers. If we ignore the whispers, we get pebbles of warnings. If we still don't pay attention, we get bricks of problems, and if we're really hard-headed, eventually the entire brick wall comes crashing down. This is a pattern I've seen repeated so often in my life that I know if you don't pay attention to the pebbles, it's just a matter of time until the bricks show up.'

She watches the sunrise when she can

'I drove to the top of the Haleakala Crater (in Hawaii) and watched the sun rise. You get to watch the day slowly unfold above the clouds. The sun casts a pink haze. It's so still up there I could feel the depth and potential of my own existence. Every sunrise is a wonder. I forget that sometimes when I get caught up in deadlines, obligations and expectations. No matter what our troubles, when the earth turns on its axis one more time, you have one more day.'

She reads

'I build a fire, turn off my BlackBerry and I'm ready to read. I can't imagine where I'd be or who I'd be had reading not been such a fundamental tool in my life. Books for me have always been a way to escape. I now consider reading a good book, a sacred indulgence.'

She takes responsibility

'I had recognised for a long time that I was responsible for my life, that every choice produced a consequence. But often the consequences seemed so out of line with my expectations. That's because I was thinking one thing but intending another. My intention of always trying to please other people, for example, produced an unwanted consequence: I often felt taken advantage of. My intention to please had the consequence that others came back and wanted more! Whatever your situation is you have created a major role in setting it up so I always ask myself "what is my real intention?" and "how have your intentions produced the experiences I'm having now?"'

She thinks twice before she buys anything

'When I moved away from home, I was $1,800 in debt within a year. I felt I'd failed. I paid off the debt and vowed never again to create more bills than I could pay. I hated the way overspending made me feel – anxious. You know you're shopping smart when you bring home a new purchase and there's no tinge of remorse, and whatever you got feels better to you ten days later than it did when you bought it.'

Three
Regaining balance

Make that mythical work–life
balance a reality.

Ten minutes to a work–life balance

Have you ever met anyone who felt they had achieved the perfect work–life balance? Probably not. Here is your chance to make that person you.

One of the most pernicious things about our stressed-out culture is that we don't notice how it switches attention away from what we value and love in life until it's too late. So here are some clues to work out if stress is stomping all over your work–life balance.

1. Do you feel like your day is spent dealing with difficult people and difficult tasks?
2. Do you feel that those you love don't have a clue what's going on with you and you don't have a clue what's going on with them?
3. Do you regularly make time for activities that nourish your soul?
4. Do you feel you could walk out the door and nobody would notice you were gone until the mortgage had to be paid?

Yes, you guessed it. Number 3 was the trick question. Answer yes to that one and you are probably all right. Answer yes to the rest and you and calm are probably strangers to each other.

In a nutshell: make sure you're putting time and effort into the people and activities that make your heart sing and it really is very difficult not to feel calm.

But perhaps in your life, too much emphasis is put on the stress caused by the 'work' part of the equation and not enough placed on the stress caused by the 'life' bit. Everyone assumes that all we need is less work, more life, and all would be harmonious balance.

Yet where it's gone wrong for many of us, especially women, is that they've cleared enough time for the 'life' part of the equation but not taken into account that that time is neither restful, nor particularly enjoyable. Research shows that men's stress hormones tend to fall when they get home whereas women's stay high long after the working day is over, presumably because they get home to confront a dozen chores and hungry kids. Your children may be the reason you get out of bed in the morning but spending time with them is not necessarily any less stressful than work – in fact, it could make work look like a walk in the park.

More time with our kids is not necessarily the answer.

More time with yourself, very probably, is.

The old saying is true: if you don't look after yourself, you can't look after anyone else. And all it takes is just 10 minutes a day.

Ten minutes of selfishness every day is enough to make a profound difference in your ability to achieve a life balance that works (more of that in the next idea). Begin to get into the habit of reviewing your day. If you didn't find 10 minutes where you actively put aside time to enjoy your life (slumping in front of the TV doesn't count), consider that day a failure. Mark it with a cross in your diary, and keep doing this until those crosses get few and far between.

The other side of the life–work balance equation is not just finding time for yourself, it's finding time for what's important. It can be helpful to think about the roles you play in life and list them: spouse, parent, employee, sister, daughter, friend, housekeeper, governor, student, etc. Next, prioritise this list in terms of the most important role. Then

Feel good now: *Spend 10 minutes every evening planning your next day. It's proven that you get one fifth more work done if you review what you want to accomplish the next day in advance. Plus what you do achieve will likely be of higher quality.*

rewrite the list in terms of what gets more of your time. Interesting? For most of us, our greatest amounts of time will be devoted to roles which are not so high on our list of priorities.

Let's get real about this. You can't devote more time out of every day to your children than your job – they have to go to school after all. But if you are regularly missing story-time because you're at work or socialising, something's gone awry in your life and having this list can help you see exactly what that is. If your sister or brother hasn't heard from you in a while, you might discover to your surprise that spending 10 minutes calling them for a catch-up makes the rest of your working day go a lot more smoothly.

Rid yourself of the disease to please

A huge amount of stress is caused by the inability to say 'no'. Many women simply don't even realise that by never saying 'no' they are saying 'yes' to much that they are completely uninterested in.

You have to lead your own life. If you don't, someone else will lead it. That may work well for a while but inevitably it will lead to stress. Of course, now and then, all of us have to do things that don't benefit us, but if for you it's a daily occurrence it's time to take back control of your own life.

Read the following statements and decide whether each is true or false for you.

- I can't relax until I finish all the things I have to do T/F
- If I didn't help out other people, I would find it hard to think much of myself T/F
- I seldom say 'no' to a work colleague or family member who needs help T/F
- I often find myself changing my own plans to fit in another task T/F
- I rarely, if ever, feel comfortable with what I've accomplished T/F
- I often feel I'm so exhausted that I don't have time for my own interests T/F
- I feel guilty relaxing T/F
- I find myself saying 'yes' to others when inside a voice is shouting 'no'. T/F
- I honestly believe that if I stop doing things for others they'd think less of me T/F

• I find it hard to ask other people to do things for me. T/F

Add up the number of Ts you scored. If your score is between 7 and 10, you think it more important to please others than please yourself. If it's between 4 and 6, you should be careful. You're veering that way. If you scored less than 3, you are good at balancing your needs with others.

Make a list of your top 10 'nos'. What do you want to eliminate from your life. Start each sentence 'I will no longer...'

Think of the top 10 situations where you need to say 'no' in order to improve your life. Now imagine yourself in these situations saying 'no'. Use this situation of you refusing an invitation when it is inconvenient as a script where A is the person to whom you want to say 'no'.

A:	*Will you come for a coffee now.*
You:	*Thank you and no.*
A:	*But we have to talk.*
You:	*You could be right and I still say thanks and no.*

The thank you makes it gracious. The no is very strong because you don't justify, defend or make excuses. The natural way would be to say 'thank you but no', try it with the 'and' instead. It's stronger: there's something in that 'but' which is more likely to cause offence and is somehow less effective.

Practise this in front of a mirror. It makes it a lot easier to do it in real life.

Remember anytime that you feel 'I should say yes', rather than 'I really want to do this', you are on the wrong track. Say no.

When someone is trying to persuade you to do things you don't want to do, the phrase that's your best friend is 'you could be right'. Admitting that you can see the other person's point of view but still resolutely saying 'no' to changing your plans makes you both right. It's a win-win.

Leave the office on time

Take control. Don't let your working day be
hijacked by others. The secret is to have your
goals clear in your mind.

Think weekly, then daily

Don't be a slave to a daily to-do list. See the big picture. On Monday morning lose the sinking 'I've got so much to do' sensation. Instead, think 'What are my goals for this week?' Decide what you want to have done by Friday and then break each goal into smaller tasks that have to be undertaken to achieve all you want by Friday. Slot these tasks into your working week, a few each day. This helps you prioritise that the tricky or difficult things, or tasks that depend other people's input, are dealt with in plenty of time. Concentrate on only three of your items on your to-do list at once so you avoid being overwhelmed.

Work with your energy cycles

Some of us operate better in the morning, some in the late afternoon. If your job demands creativity, block out your most creative periods so that you can concentrate on your most creative projects. Don't allow that time to be impinged upon by dull phone calls that could be done anytime.

Calm communication

Make the phone call you're dreading. That call you're avoiding is sapping your confidence, sense of calm and energy. Just do it.

Have meetings in the morning. People are frisky and tend to want to skip through business. Those in the afternoon drag on because we're lethargic.

Check emails just three times a day, and not necessarily first thing in the morning (that way you can end up spending a productive time responding to other people's agenda and/or chatting with friends). Don't use email as a distraction.

Limit phone calls. Talk to other people when it suits you, not them. The most time-effective way of using the phone is to limit your calls to three times a day. Make a list of calls you have to make that day and get them out the way first thing. If someone isn't there, leave a message and unless it's urgent, ask them to call you back at your next 'phone period'. Just before lunch is good. That means neither of you will linger (and you always have an excuse to end the call). Your other 'phone time' should be around 4.30 p.m. for the same reason. Of course, you can't limit phone calls completely to these times but when other people call you outside your phone times you can tell them unless it's urgent that you are in the middle of something and that you'll be free just before lunch or at the end of the working day. If you are polite and apologetic, most people offer to call you back then thus saving you the hassle of calling them.

The point is to keep phone calls shorter and put them in the context of a busy working day. Social chat is important but most of us spend too much time on it and it disrupts the flow of our thoughts concerning work.

Time restrictions stop us rambling on. This is especially true of personal calls. When a friend phones, use the above techniques, or check your clock and allow 5 minutes before making your excuses.

Even better, save personal calls as a treat for a hardworking morning.

Feel good now: *Get into the habit of underpromising. A lot of stress is of our own making because we commit ourselves to impossible schedules. Always underpromise and your boss will be delighted to get that report in a day earlier than expected, and your friend will be ecstatic that you make the party you thought you couldn't attend.*

Have a holiday at your desk

By adding grace and glamour to your everyday life, you remove stress. You can have a 'holiday of the mind' even on the most mundane day.

Reboot your commute

Give your journey to work an overhaul. Instead of a boring waste of time, reframe it as a learning experience (download language lessons onto your MP3 player); a workout (buy a pedometer and walk for some of the route); a creative project (write a page of freehand prose on the journey).

Dress mindfully

Every day select some item of clothing that makes your heart sing – a colour you love, a piece of jewellery that reminds you of good times, an outfit that makes you feel gorgeous.

Boost your environment

What five changes would make your work environment more pleasant. Clear it out, clean it up, beautify it with flowers and uplifting images. Everyday find a way to make your workplace more pleasant.

Take a break mid-afternoon

Go for a short walk in the sunshine, take a nap if you can. Or simply palm your eyes in your hand for a few minutes and visualise a calm and beautiful place. Then eat an orange – a great antidote to mid-afternoon slump.

The journey home

Create a different vibe on the way home from the morning to emphasise that you are in transition between work and play. This should be all about relaxation. Play slower tunes, and any 'thinking time' should be devoted to relaxing topics like planning your next holiday. Read cheerful novels rather than work tomes.

Get the bigger picture

The moment you stop long enough to start reviewing your life is the time you begin a process of change.

© Jackee Holder

The Wheel of Life Tree is the perfect tool to pinpoint any areas in your life that could do with some attention and thus bring balance to your life.

Before you get started, invest in a packet of colouring pencils or box of crayons. Using colour helps waken up the right hand side of the brain, the creative side. And why shouldn't bringing balance to your life be a creative act.

You'll need a copy of a blank Wheel of Life Tree: feel free to photocopy the one in this book. Begin by deciding which areas of your life each of the eight wheels represents. This is not just about choosing areas that are all sorted but also about the areas you'd like to make better. Here are some ideas for areas you might include.

- Career and Life Purpose
- Finances and Money
- Home and Environment
- Health and Well-being
- Leisure and Social Time
- Relationships and Friendships
- Spirituality and Religion
- Creativity and Inspiration
- Travel and Adventure
- Personal Style and Fashion

These are just suggestions. You'll know better than anyone what areas to include on your list. Use the eight lines at the bottom of the tree to label each of the wheels so you know what areas of your life they relate to.

Now's your chance to consider just how well each area is actually working. Don't worry, this is not about emerging with a glowing assessment. Very few of us make it to that place of perfect balance. In fact, the more honest you are, the better.

Each of the rings in each life wheel represents a sliding scale running from 1, which is the centre ring, to 5, which is the final ring at the edge of each wheel. If you rate an area of your life as a 1, it means that overall you're not happy with that area and recognise that there's room for lots of improvement. So shade in one ring only. Colouring or shading in three rings from the centre reflects the parts of this area that are working well but you know with a bit more input it could be even better. Colouring in all five rings means you feel fulfilled and satisfied with this area of your life (in which case give yourself a pat on the back).

By the way, have you noticed how relaxing colouring is and how it actually slows you down? As you colour or shade in each life wheel, be honest. Remember this is for your eyes only. Your tree will quickly identify the areas not getting as much attention as you'd like and the areas that are working just fine. Right now you might want to ask yourself: 'What actions can I take to regain balance?'

Is your tree full of colour or lacking in a particular colour?

Would you consider this a tree in the winter of its life? A tree in its autumn? Or a tree in full bloom? What does each wheel tell you about the overall health of that area of your life right now? Write a list of actions for each wheel that will help you improve the quality of each area. It's a good idea to focus on one area at a time so you don't get overwhelmed. As you make progress don't forget to colour in another ring. You can complete a new Wheel of Life Tree in three or six months' time to see how your tree may have changed.

It can feel disheartening doing this exercise. You may feel your tree is dull or lacking in much that's positive but at least now you're fully aware and engaged with what isn't working and you're in a great position to do something about it. Concentrate on the action you're going to take over the coming weeks and months. It helps to focus on one area at a time. Small changes done over time add up and often have an impact on other areas, so learn to be patient; it will serve you well. It may be more rewarding to also include areas that are working well. Positive reinforcement is good. On days when you're not feeling great, just being reminded about what is working well in your life can be extremely motivating. It's not realistic to think you'll have everything sorted out in one go.

Quiz:
Are you there for those who care?

Nearly all of us would say family and friends were the most important things in our lives. But it's all too easy for that basic truth to get lost under pressure. This quiz is a snapshot of how much time you have for what's important in your present life and can act as a wake-up call that it's time to put into practice some of the ideas in this section.

- You have forgotten a good friend's birthday *(score 1)*
- You have forgotten your mother's birthday or needed prompting *(score 2)*
- You have forgotten your partner's birthday or needed prompting *(score 3)*
- You have forgotten your child's birthday or needed prompting *(score 4)*

- In the last year, you've cancelled a personal lunch or dinner appointment at less than 24-hours' notice because you're too busy *(score 1)*
- You nearly always cancel personal appointments because you're too busy *(score 2)*
- You have significantly cut down on socialising to the point that it is nearly non-existent because there was never the time *(score 3)*
- In the last year, a good friend has said she or he would like to see more of you but it never really happened *(score 1)*
- In the last year, more than one good friend or family member has said they'd like to see you more but you are never around *(score 2)*
- In the last year, your partner has said that he or she feels you're too busy for them *(score 3)*
- You feel you have more in common with work colleagues than friends outside work *(score 1)*
- You often feel a little bored in the company of your friends *(score 1)*
- You feel you have more in common with people you work with than people at home *(score 2)*
- You feel distant from those at home *(score 2)*
- You sometimes feel guilty about how little you are involved in your family's life *(score 3)*

A score of 0

Means you may be busy but the busyness of your life doesn't seem to be affecting the quality of your relationships.

A score of 3 or less

Means that some element of busy-ness is affecting your personal relationships. It might be worth putting some extra attention into the areas of your life that the quiz has helped pinpoint.

Any more than 3

Means that it really is time to slow down and take time to nurture your relationships.

The questions are grouped so that you can see areas where you can immediately make improvements. The first section is a litmus test for 'caretaking' relationships, the very nuts and bolts of connection. The second is about prioritising relationships over other calls on your time. The third is about social isolation. (Hint: when we find other people boring it's usually a clue that we've become so wrapped up in our world that *we* have grown really boring.)

Work on your life

The aim of this idea is really simple: you'll carve out the time in your busy schedule to meet with yourself, on a regular basis – and 'coach' yourself to achieve the life you want.

The first habit you're asked to cultivate is to set up regular meetings with yourself where you'll get into the habit of engaging in quality time to think and what entrepreneur Michael E. Gerber, author of *The E-myth Revisited*, describes as not just working in your life but working *on* your life.

Before you even think about talking yourself out of it, how about getting your diary out right now and scheduling in your first coaching session? Work out when in your day would be the best time to meet up with you. Look for a time in the day when you have the most energy and are most unlikely to be distracted. It could be early morning between 5 and 7 a.m. But maybe around 9 p.m. after the children have gone to bed works better for you. It helps to plan ahead so why not write your next four sessions in your diary now? Once it goes into your diary it gives it greater importance.

It's a good idea to have your sessions at the same time and anything less than 10 minutes won't really work (otherwise you might as well stay in bed).

You may also find that having a trigger in place is a helpful reminder for your coaching sessions. You could set an alarm on your watch or mobile phone, leave yourself a voicemail message or send yourself a text. Or your stimulus for your sessions might be the aroma of a cup of coffee at a certain time each day, which becomes your trigger. Once you've sat down with your steaming cup of coffee (alone) a few times, your brain will get the signal that you are about to spend some time thinking about you. Don't forget to change your triggers after two or three months when they start being not so effective.

What do you do? Simply sitting quietly for 10 minutes or spending time writing in your notebook is all you need to do – you may be amazed at how difficult it is to be still. But it will soon become second nature and then essential to you.

Give yourself regular time and space to think

There are no restrictions as to where you hold your solo sessions. Hold them in bed (as long as you're in bed alone), parked up in your car, on a park bench, in a crowded café, in the bath or on the top of a double-decker bus. One of your goals will be getting used to hearing your own thoughts and drilling down to your own inner wisdom.

You'll only retrieve that wisdom (great ideas will eventually emerge on the tail-end of a whole bunch of rubbish ones) once you give yourself regular time and space to think.

Try it right now. Don't do anything for the next 10 minutes. Just sit quietly and be. When the 10 minutes is up, ask yourself this question: 'In that time, what is the one thought that came to me that was useful?' Write it down. The more you cultivate time to think, the more benefits you'll gain.

You may well be still dubious? The more resistance you feel to this idea, the more you may benefit from it. Give it a go. Challenge yourself to sit still for 10 minutes for the next 7 days. What have you got to lose? And you may be absolutely amazed at the difference it makes to your productivity and happiness.

Avoid the perfection trap

Your need to 'get it perfect' isn't about perfection. It's about staying in control and that isn't conducive to living a calm life.

What is your image of a calm life? Close your eyes and envision it. Chances are that your daydreams don't include clutter, disorder, your sociopathic boss or your 'fat' clothes. No, our calm life is always inextricably twinned with our perfect life. Which means we can't be calm until we get perfect. But ironically, we're so busy rushing around trying to get perfect we never get calm.

All of us like things to be 'nice', but if we can't switch off because we have to have a clean house, clear desk or an empty ironing basket before we go to sleep, then we're pretty well doomed to disappointment. You can't stop being stressed until you stop putting yourself under continual stress. Let go. Get calm.

If inside you there is a voice keeping up a constant stream of criticism telling you that you should be doing more, earning more or looking better, then chances are perfectionism is getting in the way of you living a calm life. Only you can learn to ignore that voice. But that isn't easy. Often that voice belongs to someone we know, often someone who brought us up, or who lives with us, who has no idea of the complexities of our world. If it's someone who brought you up, the chances are that they didn't have the same choices that you have and in their world it was possible to fulfil one role 'perfectly'. In your world, you can't do it all perfectly and even if you did, you still wouldn't be happy. Give it up!

Having said that, it isn't easy. Losing the fear of the person who made you this way is a big task but just recognising that it is their voice and their values and there is no rational reason for you to pay any attention to a voice that makes you miserable is a liberating experience. Even if as a child you enjoyed colour-coding your books, accept that you wouldn't be this way if someone somewhere didn't have high expectations of you. Accept something pretty basic: if you haven't earned their unconditional approval by now, you probably never will. Let it go. And if you can't, seek out a therapist to help you.

Emergency tactics

Keep your to-do list to just seven items. This is a piece of Chinese wisdom. They believe any more and you begin to get stressed out and beat yourself when you don't complete them. Stick to the main seven and don't add any more until they're done.

Ration your perfectionist behaviour. You won't probably lose it completely but only allow yourself to spend one night a week ironing until 11.30 p.m. or answering emails at midnight.

Walk barefoot in the park

Remember Jane Fonda begging Robert Redford to stop being a stuffed shirt and to walk barefoot in Central Park? Find your own equivalent and learn the amazing truth that will set you free – no one actually cares whether or not you are perfect – except you, and the person who made you this way and we've dealt with that already. The rest of the world is too busy getting on with their business to worry about yours. Whatever your version of mad, devil-may-care spontaneity – letting your roots show, leaving the kids in front of the TV for a whole Saturday to give you a break, feeding your guests shop-bought pudding – just go right ahead and be as devil-may-care as you like. The world will not implode.

Remember these wise words 'The question should be, is it worth trying to do, not can it be done?'

Jennifer Aniston's steps to calm

She turns her home into a personal sanctuary

'If I don't have a home base, I can't ground myself. I want my home to be peaceful, warm and inviting. I want to give people an experience when they come in.'

She does yoga three times a week for 30 minutes

'Yoga makes you feel strong. Inner strength. I love it!'

She has built a strong support network

'I've always wanted to have good friendships and I was inspired to create them by watching my mom with her girlfriends.' She reputedly never forgets a friend's birthday.

She's in tune with nature

She's building her dream eco-home by the sea in Malibu and has always felt most at home on the beach 'I'm an Aquarian,' is her explanation.

Hug your home

Our environment has so much influence on how
we feel. Here is how to create the perfect space –
and keep it that way.

Blitz your home in a weekend

Decluttering. Space clearing. Essential skills. Life gets slower when you give it room. Get rid of your clutter and you're free to redefine yourself. Life becomes a lot simpler. Nothing makes you feel so serene and in control of your life as chucking out stuff you don't need.

Chuck it out, lose the guilt

How does it work? Most of us live among piles of ancient magazines, defunct utensils, clothes that neither fit nor suit us. The Chinese believe that all these unlovely, unwanted things lying about haphazardly block the flow of energy – the chi – in our homes. My theory is that by losing them, we lose a ton of guilt – guilt that we'll never fit into those hellishly expensive designer jeans again, guilt that we spent all that money on skis when we only go skiing once a decade, guilt that we never cook those fabulous dinners in those two dozen cookbooks. You get the point. Just about everything in your home probably engenders some sort of guilt. Cut your belongings by a sizeable percentage and you do the same to your guilt.

The big clear-up

'Useful or beautiful.' 'Useful or beautiful.' That's the mantra. If any single object doesn't fulfil one of these criteria, bin it. Cultivate ruthlessness. If you haven't worn it, used it or thought about it in a year, do you really need it?

Have three bin bags to hand as you work. One for stuff to chuck out, one for stuff to give to charity, one for things you want to clean or mend. Visit the charity shop as soon as you can – make it a priority. Give yourself two weeks to tackle the 'mend or clean' bag – then chuck.

Do you have something which is neither useful nor beautiful, but that you don't want to get rid of for sentimental reasons? Put it away for a year. Time out of sight makes it easier to get rid of.

Do this little but often. Try a couple of one-hour sessions per week. I operate the 40–20 rule: 40 minutes graft followed by 20 minutes sitting around feeling virtuous. You get better at decluttering. Soon it's second nature. Do a couple of sessions a month. Or you could try the 'one in, one out' rule. Every time you buy something new, get rid of something old.

Importantly, find a home for everything you own. You're allowed one drawer that acts as a glory hole for all the odd items.

Get on top of housework forever

It's hard to change when your home is filthy.
And even if it's clean, keeping it that way often
means you're working until midnight.

There is no secret to having a fragrant, immaculate home. It takes time – either yours, or your cleaner's. But even if you have a cleaner, at the end of the day we all have to do a bit of cleaning – unless we've got the luxury of a housekeeper 24/7.

So here are some ideas for making housework stress a thing of the past. It will benefit two groups of people:

- The owner of a messy home – your house will be cleaner
- The owner of an immaculate home, but the price for it is you find yourself polishing kitchen units at midnight. This will help you slow down, and cut down the amount of cleaning you do. Your challenge will be to find other things to fill the great gaping holes in your schedule. You can skip through the first bit snorting.

Always have a clean kitchen sink

This seems such a petty thing, but it can make a huge difference. With a shiny sink, you feel you're in control. A shiny sink reflects back a vision of yourself as a domestic goddess (or god) in stunning control of your world. Don't leave home or go to bed for the evening without clearing the sink. It really is best to clear your kitchen straight after the evening meal – or get your kids to do it. Before bed you can't always be bothered and it sets the morning off to a bad start.

Adopt the laser beam approach

Divide your home into clearly defined areas. You will clean one of these areas thoroughly every week. No area should take more than an hour. This could look like: hallway and bathroom; kitchen; reception rooms; bedroom and spare bedroom; children's bedrooms. Now make a list of what you need to do to each area to get it cleaned. Keep a master list for each room in a file. The reason for this? With a list you get to tick off items and that's immensely satisfying. First thing Saturday morning is a good time to clean, not least because if you have children they can get involved.

Scheduling superficial cleaning

Take time to schedule in the superficial cleaning you do to keep your home bearable. It takes an hour a week – or you can split it up into 10 minutes morning and evening, three times a week. That on top of the hour a week I spend on one area is usually enough to keep your home clean, although you might need more time if your home is big. During the 10-minute sessions you could sweep and mop floors, vacuum, dust, clean bathroom, polish all reflective surfaces, get rid of all rubbish, purge magazines, empty contents of recycling bins.

Instigate the family 'scan'

Before they go to bed, ask each child to walk around each public room, scanning for their own stuff, and put away their own belongings. Start this early enough and it will become second nature. Kids cause havoc in the average home. Be aware that it's really difficult for children to keep stuff tidy if they have too much of it. Regularly cull their toys and books every six months. When they are little, do this while they're out, keep the bag for a month and only return items they appear to notice are missing. Dump the rest. As they get older children can enjoy donating to charity and it teaches them the importance of recycling.

Feel good now: *Feeling hot and bothered? Run cold water over your wrists for a few seconds.*

Zap those piles

Do you live with avalanches of paper? Here's how to get rid of the general detritus of twenty-first-century life and some ideas on finding a filing system that works.

Step 1

Gather together everything that you will need to create order in your world. Folders, pens, labels, staplers, a couple of hardback address books (personal and business) and a huge industrial strength bin bag. I also keep the family calendar and my diary at hand so I can put dates directly into them as I reveal the invites and school dates in my pile.

Step 2

Work systematically. You are going to go from one side of your desk to the other, or one side of the room to the other. Gather together one pile of paper and assorted junk and place it bang in the middle of the room or your desk. Start sorting. Every single piece of paper that you touch must be actioned.

- *If it contains a phone number that you might need in the future, then put the number straight into one of your address books.*

- *If it is a bill that has to be paid, or anything which must be started on immediately, then create a file for urgent and unpaid bills.*
- *If it's an article or piece of information that you might need in the future but which is not urgent, start creating files for these (named files) such as 'pensions', 'holidays', 'general interest'.*
- *If it is a piece of information that you need to act on or read or make a decision on but not now, put it in a file marked 'to do' and make an appointment in your diary sometime in the next week when you'll deal with it. This file should be somewhere accessible and you should clear it not less than once every two weeks or it gets out of control.*

Step 3

Keep a tickle book. Tickle as in 'tickle my memory'. This is a hardbacked notebook in which you note down the names of anything you might need in the future; the point is that you don't have to hold onto endless bits of paper just in case you ever need the information on them. In your tickle book you have enough to trace what you need. The tickle book means you can throw out dozens of pieces of paper almost as soon as they reach the desk.

Q and A: Maintaining calm at home

I can clear up piles but I can't maintain order because of the sheer volume of reading matter I'm supposed to get through to be on top of my field. How can I keep the paper under control?

Don't read business magazines or journals cover to cover. Scan the contents, choose three articles that seem most important. Tear them out. Bin the rest. Carry the articles with you in your briefcase and read them in 'down time' such as on your commute.

How long should I keep bank statements and the like?

As a rule, in the UK, you should keep bank statements and credit card statements for two years and anything to do with the tax office for six years. Most importantly in these days of identity theft, shred or burn your statements.

I've followed your ideas but now it's done, why not just get a cleaner?

Having a cleaner whose standards are lower than your own doesn't help – and it's amazing how many people are in that boat. At the end of the day, you have to do some cleaning yourself. The best advice is to make sure they clean – and you tidy. It's not his or her job to unload the dishwasher. Their job is to prioritise the cupboards you haven't seen inside for decades and get stuck into the corners you're always too busy to do. Paying your cleaner to pick up your kids' toys probably isn't the best use of her time or your money.

I have tons of expensive stuff that I can't bear to just chuck even though I know I don't want it.

That is fear talking. Fear that if you give away the £500 suit you've worn twice, you'll never get another one. But it's that very suit hanging in your wardrobe reproaching you that stops you looking around for something that would suit you better. Get rid of the suit and a better one will take its place, one that you might possibly wear. Or something else will happen. You'll change, you'll have a lifestyle that only calls for jeans and the suit will be redundant.

Staying calm around difficult people

Stress is other people. Here's how to deal with the energy black holes.

All around you are people who are unhappy, negative, or angry and who would like nothing more than to drag you into their stressful world. And there is absolutely nothing you can do about them. The only thing you can change is your attitude. (There is a proviso to this – if your life is littered with difficult people out to get you, then it may be something to do with your expectations.)

Some black holes are strangers

Other people have their own agenda. You can't know what they are and you can't change them. Take a tip from Rosamond Richardson, author and yoga teacher. She recommends visualising yourself surrounded by white light, creating a protective bubble around you. Negativity just bounces off this white light and can't affect you. You don't have to believe this for it to work. The more you visualise the bubble, the better it works.

Some black holes share your life, your home, your bed…

Don't waste a moment dwelling on how less stressful life would be if John would only be kinder, Mum would cheer up a bit, Emil was more help around the home, or your boss was less aggressive.

This is a surprisingly telling little exercise that you can do in five minutes on the back of a napkin. It may give you a shock. Make a list of the people with whom you have regular contact. Then divide that list into three categories.

- The energisers. They look after you in every way. They give great advice. They bring happiness to your life.
- The neutral. They're OK. Neither great nor bad.
- The drainers. They're users, people who don't deliver, let you down, bring you down. They also include gossips, sexists, racists, bitches (of both sexes), or anyone at all who leaves you with a bad feeling after a meeting for whatever reason.

It's simple when you recognise this. Maximise your time with the energisers. Look for them when you enter a room and gravitate towards them whether you've been introduced or not. We all know these people when we meet them. If you have too many neutrals, think how you can bring more energisers into your life.

And the drainers? Your time with them should be strictly limited and if some of them are your closest friends, your family, your lover, you need to think about that closely. You may feel unable to cut them out now (although this is an option) but you can limit the time that you allow them to suck you into their world.

If your drainers are at work, pitch up, work hard, do your best. Be kind. That's all you can do. You may change the culture and if you can't, look for a new job. If you look around and see nothing but drainers, could it be that you get something out of being the caring counsellor. Try changing the dynamic of your relationship: limit time with them; do lovely things when you're with them; try changing the conversation to more pleasant subjects. If you persist with this, they will either raise their game or drop you. If you find it impossible to stay upbeat around them, then you will have to decide what is more important to you; your role as carer or having a calm life.

What's your Plan B?

Take the insecurity out of your life. Plan Bs are
your best friends when it comes to inducing
calm even when the going gets rough.

Deciding on Plan B

The life you're living is Plan A. Plan B is what happens if it all goes pear-shaped. Know how you'd get from A to B and you remove a huge chunk of the stress that is caused by worry about the future.

Every life has its fair share of upsets and reversals of fortune. An essential of the Plan B is to be able to look at your life dispassionately and see potential stress lines – where your life is likely to come apart. For instance:

- If you work in a volatile industry, it's work. Your Plan B is what you'll do if you lose your job
- If your relationship is struggling, your Plan B is what you'll do if you split up.
- If your health isn't good, your Plan B is to research methods of financing life if bad stuff happens.

Someone once said that worrying is praying for a negative outcome. Please don't think this is about wishing negative outcomes into being. You might love your Plan A, but you should equally love your Plan B. Plan Bs are your choice and they should be inspiring to you as much as Plan A if not more so. They don't work to calm you otherwise.

Thinking about it is just planning for an alternative life that you would love to live. You may never use your Plan B in which case it's a lovely fantasy. But you may find that planning for it is so alluring that you actively enjoy it. And it's a wonderful comfort blanket, a great place to sink into when real life is a bit stressful. On those horrid nights when you wake up and can't get to sleep because of catastrophic

You may never use your Plan B in which case it's a lovely fantasy

thoughts swirling in your brain; you know those nights? Well, with a Plan B, you worry for about 30 seconds, go 'Oh, I remember, I've got a plan B,' roll over and doze off again.

But for Plan B to work on this level, it has to be a fantasy built on reality. It can't be as vague as 'I'll sell the house and move to France'. It should be way more concrete.

Building the dream

First, decide on your Plan B and start a file. Add cuttings, pictures, information to it. Suppose you were going to sell your house and move to France. Your file for this would include information on people who had done the same thing, and research on how much you'd need to live on per year, with concrete plans of how to raise that. If you have children, you'd also need to research the education system. Book those French lessons now. Exactly which parts of France interest you most?

Your Plan B should be realistic but it should be awesome. It shouldn't be a case of 'Oh well, I could always move back in with Mum'. It should be training to become a chef, starting your own business, backpacking around Bolivia. It should make your heart sing. Plan realistically but dream big.

Building an emergency fund

Think about the financial position you'd need to be in to make it work, and take steps to achieve it. The ideal sum for a 'just in case' fund is 8 months of living expenses. Go through your bank statements adding up your essential outgoings for a year – this is truly frightening – take the total, divide by 12 and then multiply by 8.

Still reeling? OK, 8 months is ideal but it's that – an ideal. However, for anyone who wants to feel calm in the face of disaster, three months is essential. That's the bare minimum you should have in an easily accessible savings account. Start one today and pay into it by direct debit.

What happens when you spend more of your time thinking about Plan B than worrying about Plan A? Terrific, then it's time to move your life on.

Feel good now: *Choose a task that you're not looking forward to. First remember that whether or not you do the task is your choice. Now imagine having completed the task and how much you enjoyed doing it. Feel the pleasure of having completed it. Next, set aside a time to do the task. Remember that you choose your thoughts, so it's down to you whether you feel depressed or energised about the task. If you feel depressed, the task will become more of a chore and the quality of the thinking you put into it will be reduced.*

The CREATE model

When life isn't going well, The CREATE model ensures you have a map that will help you stay on track.

The model comprises the following steps:

- *Challenge and create*
- *Reframe and replace your negative thinking*
- *Engage and energise*
- *Act and award*
- *Tools and techniques*
- *Explore and evaluate*

Challenge and create

What challenges are you up against? You'll recognise challenges as those areas of your life that don't function well or where you feel drained or stretched. Once you face your challenges square on, it's surprising how much better you'll feel. Whatever the challenge – drink, debt, a relationship, being disorganised – at the very least be willing to tell yourself the truth. Why? Because once you own up to it then you can get on with the business of transforming it. Make a note of your challenges in writing. Without knowing how this will be achieved, take each challenge separately and ask yourself, 'If I had to create a different experience in this area of my life what would it look like?' Make a list of your new positive outcomes for each of your challenges.

Reframe and replace your negative thinking

Get into the habit of reframing and replacing your negative thoughts and beliefs. Say you find your inner thoughts telling you, 'Oh, you'll never be any good as a manager', interrupt these thoughts by asking yourself this question: 'Is this belief or thought moving me towards positive action or negative action?' If the answer is towards negative action then set about convincing yourself of the opposite. List all the reasons why you'd make a good manager and keep repeating these to yourself regularly and consistently. To reinforce the reasons write them down. Like your old habit, this new habit has to be practised rigorously and regularly.

Engage and energise

Start engaging with life right now, no matter how bad it is. That means no excuses. If you just learned that you're going to be made redundant then make a start right away on updating your CV. Don't make the mistake of waiting for your life to be sorted before you start having a good time. Get out there and enjoy yourself. When you start fully engaging with your life right where you are, you'll become energised, and so will your life.

Act and award

One of the most powerful ways to put life on a better path is learning to take action regardless of how you are feeling. So when you feel depressed still push yourself to turn on the computer and send one email. The mere action of sending just one email motivates you to send another one. Once you get into the habit of taking action no matter what, build giving yourself awards and acknowledgements into the process. In other words, don't let your actions go unacknowledged. Today, what action don't you feel like taking that you could make a start on right now? Do it, and notice how much stronger you feel.

Tools and techniques

Do you have a toolkit of techniques and ideas that work for you? Your toolkit is a valuable resource in your journey to becoming your own best life coach. For instance, if you find it helps to write down your feelings, notice how disconnected and tetchy you'll feel if you don't keep your journal in times of stress. Make a list of your life tools, those that support you, the ones that work and get results, and use them regularly.

Explore and evaluate

Most of the satisfaction of life comes from the journey itself rather than the destination. On top of this make a conscious effort to evaluate. Ask yourself questions, monitor your progress, record your achievements, make observations of how you navigated around obstacles and setbacks. Make sure you're a partner in your life and not an observer.

Four
Cherish yourself

Love yourself and life gets calm,
serene, easier…

Retreat and restore

Some time alone with your own thoughts is one of the best ways to relax. This idea is about obliterating the low-grade noise pollution that is now the background for most of our lives. Stop for a moment and think just how much noise is generated in your home now compared to the home you grew up in. Televisions in every room. Telephones wherever you go. Music playing where it never played before (while you shop, on the end of the phone while you wait).

This constant barrage of noise is stressful. Here is a three-step plan to give yourself a break.

Step 1: Switch off the noise

TV will eat up your life. Some nine year olds are watching up to four hours a day and these children perform less well on all measures of intelligence and achievement. TV does exactly the same thing to adults. It is such a very passive form of entertainment; it's been proven that just lying on the couch doing nothing burns off more calories than watching TV, presumably because without TV at least you're generating some thoughts in your head. Reclaim hours of your time by limiting TV to one or two favourite programmes a week. The rest of the time, switch it off. Listen to voice radio or music if you must have some noise.

Step 2: Be silent

This is difficult to manage if you live with other people. But take a day off work and experiment with no noise. No TV, no radio, no phone – switch them off. Silence really is golden. Not talking gives you the chance to listen to what your inner voice is trying to say to you.

Step 3: Retreat

The best way of doing this is to go on a dedicated retreat

– all sorts of institutions, religious or otherwise, run them. You can retreat and do yoga or dance or write or paint – or do absolutely nothing.

Of course, you don't have to leave home for that. It's much easier if you can escape but it's not impossible to put aside the hassles of everyday life and retreat in your own home. Clear away any clutter. Put away laptops, phones, diaries, PDAs, BlackBerries – all work paraphernalia should be banished. Make your house as calm, restful and serene as possible.

Seven steps to retreating

1. Set aside at least 24 hours, preferably longer. Warn everyone you know that you don't want to be disturbed.
2. If you have family, do the best you can to escape. One way of doing it is to come back on your own a day early from a break or leave a day after everyone else.
3. Get in all the food you'll need. Plan ahead. Make it especially tasty and nutritious. You don't want to have to venture out for supplies.
4. Switch off the phone. Don't open your mail.
5. Don't speak.
6. This is your opportunity to go inwards and not only

relax fully but work out what you really want. Keep the TV and radio off. Listen to music if you like but nothing too emotional. Limit reading to a few hours so you don't simply lose yourself in a book. Give your brain a chance to unravel and see what comes up.

7. Write in a journal, paint or draw, invent recipes. Do anything creative.

Better yet, be very still. Lie on the couch with a blanket and your thoughts. Breathe. Stay silent for as long as you can.

Feel good now: *A lot of stress in our relationships with other people comes from trying to second guess what they're thinking or what their intention is. Try saying: 'what other people think of me is none of my business'. Think about that statement closely. When you start believing it, life gets a whole lot easier.*

Get rid of what's not working

One of the easiest ways to increase your energy
and get great results is by the simple process
of removing tolerations (things and people that
drain your energy) from your life. So out with
the old and in with the new.

In coaching the word toleration is generally applied to areas of your life where you're putting up with something without realising the cost to you in terms of energy, wasted time spent worrying and inconvenience. Tolerations can include unfinished projects, incomplete household chores (things that either need fixing or replacing) and relationships that, when examined, leave you feeling drained. When you start to tackle your tolerations you are creating more emotional, mental, creative and physical energy that you can then use to channel into your vision and goals. Leaving them unattended – even if you don't realise it – often means that

When you're flushing out your tolerations leave no stone unturned

the tolerations will eventually hold you back or certainly hold up your progress later on down the line. That's the thing about tolerations, it's so easy not to realise just how powerful they are in holding you back.

Take a good look at your life and make a list of key areas where you might be putting up with tolerations, for example home, relationships, work, health and well-being. Brainstorm as many items, from the small to the big, under each category. Once you have generated several items under each category, decide on where to start and get to work on clearing these tolerations as quickly as you can. When you're flushing out your tolerations leave no stone unturned. Most people find it easiest to start with their physical space. Take a look around. What needs clearing or fixing? Is it the filing cupboard in your office spilling over with paper? Or is it a drawer that's full of bits of paper you rarely refer to? What about the boot of your car, the cupboard under the stairs or the spare room that you can't move in?

Keep working through your list over the next few weeks and months. It's also a good idea to get into the habit of handling your tolerations on a regular basis. With your tolerations out of the way you'll attract better opportunities because you will have cleared space for what you want in your life.

Working with the Pareto Principle

Take a look through your wardrobe. How many of the items in your wardrobe do you actually wear?

According to the Pareto Principle you wear 20% of your wardrobe and the other 80% is a waste of wardrobe space. The Pareto Principle applies to just about everything in your life. 20% of your work generates 80% of your income. You spend 80% of your time in 20% of your home. Look at areas of your life where the Pareto Principle can help you make decisions on what should go. Start to focus on the 20% that works in your life and get rid of the 80% that's a waste of space.

Quiz:
Is it time to take stress seriously?

You're stressed. But how stressed? Here are some statements worth addressing. Do you agree or disagree with the following? Answer 'yes' or 'no'.

You fantasise a lot about your perfect life that doesn't include your dull/ annoying/ partner/ job.
Score 1 for a yes

You say 'I can't take it any more' at least once a week.
Score 2 for a yes

You feel unappreciated.
Score 3 for a yes

Tension is beginning to affect your health.
Score 3 for a yes

You wake dreading the day ahead.

Score 3 for a yes

All you want to do in the evening is slump in front of the TV and/ or sleep.

Score 1 for a yes

A score of 4 or under

Mild level of dissatisfaction. This indicates that the present situation is stressful but potentially saveable.

9 or under

Life is not good and you know you need to start looking after yourself and making changes soon.

10 or over

Burnout imminent. Make beating stress your priority.

Build your team

Behind every superhero, idol, famous person, celebrity, genius or everyday person you'll find a team of people working away behind the scenes to make them who they are. What about building a team of your own?

Grab a blank sheet of paper, or the back of an envelope will do. Pop your name in the middle of the page then, according to closeness or distance, plot your circle of friends on the page. Now do the same but on this page write down the names of all the people who support and take care of you in other ways. This might include people like your hairdresser, the cleaner, your accountant, your doctor and your web designer. Your Dream Team makes it possible for you to do what you do well. Each one makes an important contribution both to your well-being and your productivity and efficiency. Quite often it's easy to ignore the value that these individuals bring to the quality of our lives.

Your Dream Team needs to include individuals better qualified to support you and your business. Don't forget to include individuals who take care of your body, your soul, your finances, your car, your teeth, your feet, your holidays, your hair and your home.

It's so important to develop good rapport with each one. At the end of the day you want everyone on your side from the handyman to the mortgage adviser.

Invest in your relationships with everyone on your team and your life should get easier as the service improves.

If you know you will never feel rapport with a particular member, isn't it time to look around for a replacement.

Now let's take a review of both your friendships and your Dream Team. Go through each name one by one and on a scale of 1–10, with 10 meaning the relationship is going really great and 1 meaning it's not so great, review each of your relationships. You can do this by asking yourself questions like: Who motivates and rocks me? Who sinks or drains my energy? Is there anyone on the list who drains my energy so much they make me ill? Is the balance right in my friendships? Is there a good flow between giving and receiving? Are my roles fluid and flexible? Your answers may point to a friendship that has fizzled out or the need to change or let go of a member of your team.

Perhaps the review will throw light on a resentment that hasn't been cleared up or the need to make a special effort to let someone know how much you care or how much their service is appreciated. Now's the time to take action.

Brainstorm to a better way

*Arrange for a group of friends to support you in resolving
a personal challenge. An hour will do fine. Arranging food
or drinks always makes the invitation a bit more inviting.
But stick to your agenda first, then socialise. Arrange
to meet in a quiet space where you won't be distracted.
In the first 10 minutes outline your challenge or issue.
The group then has 30 minutes to ask you a series of
questions or make comments. Listen and take note of the
questions and the comments. At the end take another 10
minutes to share your thoughts and reflections on what's
been said, thank your guests and close the proceedings.
This is a variation on the Quaker practice called the
Clearness Committee.*

Sigourney Weaver's steps to calm

She remembers to laugh

'We shouldn't be afraid of ageing – it has a lot to offer, especially if, like me, you weren't that good being young. I had a serious reputation and that overshadowed my natural humour, but now I feel I can indulge it. It's very relaxing not to be anxious any more.'

She can slow down

'I always had a New York kind of attitude. I had to be busy, busy, busy but now I want to be involved, engaged – not skimming the surface. I'm looking forward to eating lunch with someone I love without watching the clock. Making a meal and not rushing through it, but actually enjoying the process.'

She believes in being engaged with life

'I remember my father, who was still skiing into his eighties, and the actress Jessica Tandy who took care of herself and looked beautiful well into her nineties. She'd spend her day cooking a meal and savouring the process. They had a discipline and elegance that I admire. Staying engaged, being of service and celebrating your goofy, silly side: that's what I aspire to.'

Money is your friend

Detoxing is letting go of waste and toxins that are harmful to our system. Our attitudes to money can be harmful to our peace of mind and our long term prosperity.

Ever done a financial detox? It means facing some home truths and cleaning up your financial act.

There's a reason why we say keep an eye on the money. That's because people who have money, enjoy money and are successful with money keep close track of their money and how they spend it. So how about a little bit of financial detoxification?

It's always a good idea to start at the root of a problem because if we don't get to the root cause we're only touching the surface. Many of your challenges with money will have been embedded in what you learned about money when you were a child. Let's start by recalling the first time you remember having a negative experience around money.

Describe the experience in a few sentences in your notebook then sit back and take a few deep breaths. Now ask yourself, what did I take that experience to mean to me? Take another deep breath. Think as you are examining your financial arrangements and deep-rooted attitudes to money, is this working positively for me or is it costing me? If it's not working for me, what is the real cost to me – lack of self-esteem, guilt, lack of energy? Take a deep breath. Finish off by quickly answering this question: if I knew what changes to make to the way I handle my finances, these would be (complete the sentence).

Phew, what did you discover? Did you notice that you either mirrored or rebelled against your parents' attitude to money? Did you feel a need to forgive yourself for

Money is both an emotional and an energetic force

anything? You may start to make lots of connections; write down your observations in your notebook. They'll come in handy for the next exercise.

At this point it's a good idea to take a break. You may be finding this work around money very emotional. Money is both an emotional and an energetic force so don't be shocked by how you might be feeling. This might be a good point to give yourself a comfort treat before you continue.

Make a list of incomplete or unresolved financial issues from your past. This could be an unpaid debt or a poor financial decision. Once you have listed your issues number them. Take your top three issues and outline three steps that will mean taking action to resolve the issue.

Now get to work. It may take some weeks or even months to see results. Be patient. As you work your way through your list you may begin to uncover the reason why you misused money, overspent or disrespected friendships or family members because of money. For a while your financial detox may feel like it's making things worse rather than better. This is only a short-term experience. The work you are doing now will have far-reaching long-term

You're worth every penny of your time and investment

implications. So keep going. You're worth every penny of your time and investment.

And if you want to make amends right now, follow the example of Oprah Winfrey who recently gave each member of her audience a sum of money to do good in their communities. A management company in the US has since followed suit, giving its employees money to give away to someone else in need. Start today; give something away.

Give big

It's not just money that we give away; it's grace, too. Be an agent of change and delight for the next week. Think of ways in which you can practise random acts of kindness. Let someone go in front of you in a queue. Give up your seat on a packed train to someone who looks more tired and worn out than you. Deliver a home-cooked meal to a friend who's feeling a bit down.

A zone of your own

Imagine a place with no phone, no noise, no hassle, no problems. Peace is a state of mind, but it can also be a corner of a secluded garden, a cubby hole under the stairs, a bed that you share with no one else, or a garden shed.

Everyone needs space. It's just that we don't realise it. The need for a quiet place is universal. Why? Because in some profound way having a corner where you can let your imagination run free and where you have control is deeply important to the human spirit. As a child, did you have a secret place where you would hide away? Did you build shrines? No? Think of the times you set up your favourite toys next to your bed, your dolls aligned

Everyone needs space. It's just that we don't realise it. The need for a quiet place is universal

looking just right on a shelf, 'special' power stones hidden in a secret place only you knew about? Children love talismans and can spend hours contemplating a feather, a flower, a broken bottle. This is how they de-stress away from their parents, in a world of their own where they choose the objects that soothe them and where they decide their significance – not the grown-ups.

Creating a place where you can go that is uniquely yours, where you have chosen what you look at, what you feel, hear and smell will prove invaluable in helping you retain calm. A room is ideal, a cupboard will do, a corner of a room – just one armchair will be enough.

There you are in control and you can read, rest, dream, just be. It could be a seat in your garden, a daybed in the spare room, a dressing table or simply a shelf or windowsill that you can enjoy placing favourite objects on and admiring them.

You can seek your sanctuary in creativity. Dedicate a corner of your desk to calm. Keep on it a journal, or paints or pencils, embroidery or a favourite book. And when life gets too frantic, noisy or annoying, retreat there and nourish the deepest and more spiritual part of you.

If you are still struggling to think of a way you can make this happen, write down what taste, scent, sensations, sound and sight immediately relaxes you and place them into a beautiful box that you can pull out from under the bed whenever you need to create an immediate sense of calm. This is a portable sanctuary, you can keep it anywhere. You could have a favourite scented candle, a beautiful shawl or rug, a peaceful CD, an embroidered cushion, a sensational bar of chocolate, a book of poetry on spirituality, a scented hand cream. Whenever you open it you are making a promise to yourself to relax and nurture yourself even if only for five minutes.

Whatever sanctuary you decide on, it should be so attractive to you that you long to sink into it, that way you'll want to carve out a little time for yourself as often as possible so you can be there. And actively seeking out time to enjoy life is the essence of relaxation.

Feel good now: *Write down what taste, scent, sensation, sound and sight immediately relaxes you and gather them in one place so they are always at hand. Velvet slippers, satin quilts, birdsong, pink light, roses. What sensual pleasures calm you down instantly?*

Q and A:
Reducing stress

Stress is affecting my sleep. Are there any supplements that can help?

Passiflora and valerian have been used for millennia to sedate naturally and defuse stress. They are particularly useful to help you sleep. You can buy tablet formulations that contain these herbs at pharmacies. A simple cup of chamomile tea before bed will also help, especially if you turn it into a ritual.

Another herb, rhodiola, is good for aiding focus and concentration under stressful conditions and it could help if you are having trouble getting through the days. Students who took it reported being less stressed and less tired than those on placebo.

A lot of these ideas sound way too simple to work for me. I don't think sitting quietly and having a cup of tea will help my manic stress levels.

Get outside if at all possible. Nature works on a very deep level to help you feel 'connected'. What you are seeking is to experience being in 'flow' as it was described by famous psychologist Mihaly Csikszentmihalyi. Being in the flow means being totally absorbed in whatever it is that we are doing, at peace with ourselves and the world. Being outside helps combat that feeling of being harried and trapped by our demanding world. Breathe. Feel the weather. You're not just seeking beauty – it's a matter of connection with the bigger picture.

I've tried meditation. I can't switch my thoughts off or visualise problems drifting away as recommended.

Some people find it helps to see their thoughts passing like a parade in front of them. Others see them written down as a tickertape. Another method is to see each of your worries as a concrete image with a label stuck on it that 'names' it. Sometimes our minds work so fast that we don't even stop long enough to name those anxieties

Nature works on a very deep level to help you feel 'connected'

passing through our heads – they just become a blur of general anxiety. Practise this and you'll slow down that ceaseless twittering of anxious thoughts – what the Chinese call 'monkey' chatter.

What about massage?

Regular massage has been proven to help reduce stress levels but a lot depends on the quality of the therapist. A bad massage in disruptive surroundings can be stressful. Ask for recommendations from friends of someone good. Nothing beats falling straight into bed after a massage so if you can find someone good who can visit your home that would be perfect.

There is a form of massage – hot stone therapy – that is particularly relaxing. It involves application of hot and cold stones. It appears to work on a deep level to remove tension in the muscles.

Feel good now: *Lemon balm helps beat anxiety and irritability. You can buy lemon balm herb in supplement form at your chemist or find a supplier on the web.*

Perfect your future

Next stop, your future life. Have serious fun
creating a compelling vision for your future
that's creative and inspiring. Your future lies in
your hands.

A really good starting point is to begin with the end in mind. Think about where you want to be and begin to work your way backwards. This is as much an adventure in your creativity as it is in introducing more play and fun into your life. Go to an art or stationery shop and purchase a large

Think about where you want to be and begin to work your way backwards

sheet of poster paper, probably covering at least the size of eight A4 sheets and some glue. Gather together a range of magazines from health and lifestyle women's magazines and home and garden magazines, to computer and men's lifestyle magazines. It's important if you're buying your magazines off the shelf to have a flick through the magazines first to make sure you like the kinds of images they carry. Set aside an hour or more. Clear a space in a room and get everything out. Make sure you're wearing comfortable clothing so you can move around easily. You're going to make a collage of your future. Start off by leafing through the magazines and tearing out images, words and ideas that move you and inspire you. You don't have to worry about why you've been inspired but it might get you thinking about what areas of your life you would like that image to reflect. As you relax into the exercise you'll build up momentum. When you're doing your collage you'll probably experience what psychologists call 'the flow', being totally involved in an activity and totally focused on what you are doing in the present moment. Once you have a pile of images, start putting together your collage, using the images to reflect how you would like your life to be in the future.

Think big, think outside the box and push your own expectations about what is really possible for you.

The next step is often overlooked and yet it is an important one. What you do with your collage does make a difference.

Think big, think outside the box and push your own expectations about what is really possible for you

Think about where you'll display your collage, preferably where you can see it every day. Now the work begins of programming these images into your mind so that they become a part of you. Imagine yourself in front of your vision map. Choose one particular image or scene from your vision map. Close your eyes and imagine yourself feeling, seeing, tasting, sensing and hearing everything associated with that particular scene. When you have made your connections, imagine yourself walking backwards from the scene from your vision map into this present moment. Ask yourself what new steps and actions you will need to take to move this area of your life on to a whole new level.

Remember the words of Belle Livingstone, adventurer and writer: 'I looked always outside of myself to see what I could make the world give me, instead of looking within myself to see what was there.'

Switch off, tune out

You know how easy it is for your thoughts to spiral out of control. This exercise is about reversing the process; with a bit of direction, you can rein in your thoughts and think yourself calmer.

Feel refreshed

Imagine you are standing under a waterfall – recent research says the most relaxing way to drop off is being near a waterfall. A stream of water (warm or cool) gently cascades over your head, running downwards over the outside of your body, taking with it tensions and negative thoughts, which soak into the ground. Repeat three times. Next imagine the water is entering the crown of your head, and running through your body. Use your imagination to visualise its force cleansing your organs, joints digestive tract and so on. The idea is that the water will drain the negative thoughts and toxins out of your body through the soles of your feet and down into the earth.

Lose your worries

Visualise taking handfuls of worries out of your head and stuffing them into a hot air balloon. Imagine the colour of the balloon and set it in breathtaking scenery with blue skies and fluffy white clouds, or a stunning red and gold sunset. Undo the ties one by one and let your cares float away. Or you could visualise your worries written on pieces of paper, mentally put them in a file, close the file firmly and then lock them away in a filing cabinet.

Music to your ears

From whale music to Mozart, how to
turn on, tune in, relax.

Music is powerful and can have strong physiological effects, from improving your mood to lowering your heart rate. And one study found that 96% of people's sleep improved after listening to classical or new age music.

When you put on your favourite track, what's happening to your body? The sound goes in through your ear which sends impulses to the brain. Your brain reacts to these impulses and sends out directions that help control your heart rate, breathing, blood pressure and muscle tension. Music can even trigger the painkilling, mood-boosting chemicals endorphins. The right track can therefore slow your breathing and your heart rate, relax your muscles and put you in a great mood.

And so to bed

So what music should you be listening to? Scientific studies show that sleep is easier if you listen to classical music before bed and the expert opinion is that music to relax you before bed should be quiet, melodic, with a slow beat and few, if any, rhythmic accents. Listening to Pachelbel's Canon, for instance, at around 64 beats per minute, the rate of a resting heart beat, will slow your breathing rate and heart rate and change your brainwave pattern from rapid beta waves to the slower, sleepier alpha ones. And Mozart, which contains a lot of high notes, seems to reduce the level of adrenaline and slow the metabolism.

How to use music to change your mood

• Make a happy tape. Find three songs that sound like you feel when you are stressed or down, three that embody the sense of calm you want to feel and three in between. Burn them onto a CD, the music should gradually become calmer, quieter and slower. Put this on in the evening and it will guide you through your feelings and lift your mood.

• Let someone else do the work. There are hundreds of relaxation CDs on the market, some simply for relaxing, some for insomnia and stress. If you don't fancy music, look to nature – you can now get anything from whale and dolphin music to the sounds of waterfalls and waves crashing against the shore. If you're feeling adventurous make your own tape of relaxing sounds – walking through autumn leaves, running water, twittering birds.

• Try sound therapy. This is the theory that toning, making a sound with an elongated vowel for an extended period, can help relieve tension and relax your muscles. Apparently, every organ in our body has a certain vibration which can get out of balance – and hitting the right note can restore the balance. For a 3-minute relaxation, make a long-o (as in ocean) or ah (as in aha) sound. This helps get rid of any thoughts cluttering your mind. If the sounds of waterfalls and twittering birds aren't up your street, then you're better off playing something you like. Not everyone responds to classical music, but anything that you enjoy and find relaxing that pushes other noises, like traffic, out of your mind is going to help you sleep. If you play a piece of music that you don't like, even if it is classical, then it won't be restful. If a slow tune gives your mind time to fret or obsess, it's a waste of time. You need a livelier song to distract you.

• Once you've chosen your music, lie down quietly, taking even, deep breaths. Clear your head of all thoughts. Just let the music wash over you. Notice your heart rate lower, know your metabolism is dropping, feel your eyelids droop. Sleep.

Creating perfect moments

This is possibly the most valuable life-skill you'll ever learn. And if you're struggling to put into practice the idea of taking 10 minutes a day for yourself, then this tells you how.

The only guarantee that tomorrow will be calmer than today is if you take steps to determine it will happen. How? By taking 10 minutes to get calm, and stay that way.

We humans are not so good at predicting what will make us happy. We work hard at the 'right' job. We save for the big house and flash car. We think surely parenthood will make

Guarantee that tomorrow will be calmer than today by taking steps to determine it will happen

us really, really happy – and it does, for a while. Until our adorable toddlers grow into worrisome teens, or adorable teens – but still we're worried sick about them. Human happiness is the holy grail, but no one has yet found a formula for it.

Or have they? In the last few years, neuroscientists have moved their attention from what's going wrong in the brains of depressed people to exploring what's going right in the brains of happy people. And for the most part, it's quite simple.

Happy people don't get so busy stressing about building a 'perfect' tomorrow. They're lolling around at least some of the time having a perfect today. They create oases of calm – whether that's roller blading, enjoying a drink, watching a sunset or reading a book – right now, right here.

It turns out that the surest, indeed, the only predictor of how happy you are going to be in the future is how good you are at being happy today. If you want to know if you are going to be stressed out tomorrow, ask yourself what are you doing to diminish your stress today? And if the answer's nothing much, don't hold your breath. You are unlikely to be that calm and serene person you want to be anytime soon.

We can plan the perfect wedding, party, marriage, career. But we have absolutely no idea when we get 'there' a perfect anything is going to be delivered. The only thing we can do is guarantee, for that day at least, we will have a perfect moment – a moment of no stress, total calm, where we pursue pure joy.

What is a perfect moment for you? We've all experienced that feeling when life seems 'bigger' than ourselves. All you have to do is give yourself the space to feel it more often – ideally at least once a day.

Some people stay in this state the whole time. They're the ones we call enlightened. Some people slip into it as easily as slipping on a favourite coat. They've practised an awful lot, by allowing spontaneous opportunities to bloom into perfect moments as often as they can. Only you can know what your perfect moments will be. For you it may be waking in a sunlit, peaceful bedroom (taking the time to clear your room of clutter the night before is a pragmatic method of making sure when you open your eyes, you get a perfect moment). It could be a glass of wine as the sun dips behind the horizon, or 10 minutes dancing round the kitchen. It could be running under blossom trees in the park, or colouring in with your child, or deciding on the spur of the moment to have a latte and a slice of chocolate cake in the middle of the afternoon. Slipping between the sheets mid-afternoon for a little doze is an excellent perfect moment. Speaking of slipping between the sheets, sex is a very reliable way. Preparing, cooking, eating food is another.

Planning for your perfect moments means that they are more likely to happen. And if nothing else, at the end of the day, you'll be able to say 'for a few minutes at least, life was calm, life was good'. Enjoying life today is the only certainty you have of happiness and your best chance of being calmer tomorrow.

Remember the words of Walt Whitman: 'Happiness, not in another place but this place…not for another hour, but this hour.'

Planning for your perfect moments means that they are more likely to happen

Soon perfect moments will be perfect half hours, perfect afternoons, perfect weeks. You'll find yourself stopping just to admire the way the sunlight hits your kitchen table at that perfect angle. And then a few moments later there will be another perfect moment until they link together like a string of beads. Nothing will have changed in your world, except yourself.

Index